Rock n' Blues Harmonica

Stories, Lessons & Record Index

By
Jon Gindick

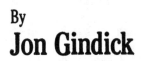

With illustrations by
Mark Zingarelli
Calligraphy by
Holly Fox
Special thanks to
Martin Eldridge
for his creative suggestions.

Cross Harp Press
San Diego—Visalia—Los Angeles

Jam-Along Cassette Lessons From The Author

Jon Gindick and the Cross Harp Press proudly present two new cassette lessons for readers of *Rock n' Blues Harmonica*.

1. Rock n' Blues Accompaniment Cassette will get you out of your chair and jamming with the very first song. This tape is designed to give you that "playing with a band" feeling as you and Jon use the Cross Harp riffs described in Chapter V to jam with bass, drums, ominchord and guitar. Featured music includes 12 bar blues with guitar, **E minor** jam, drum jam, Straight Harp, Slant Harp and more. For your **C**, **A**, and **G** harmonicas. $7.95.

2. Three Chords of the Blues Cassette is for harp players who want to hear and play the chord and riff cycles in Chapter VI of *Rock n' Blues Harmonica*. Each cycle is played slowly enough for you to understand and imitate. Improvisational Cross Harp for solo harmonica and instrumental accompaniment round out this valuable harmonica lesson. For harps in the keys of **C** and **G**. $7.95.

Lessons are $7.95 each or $14.95 for both. Guaranteed. Please send U.S. funds only. Overseas include $3.00 extra. Send your check or money order to:

> **Jon Gindick**
> **Cross Harp Press**
> **344 Ranch Road**
> **Visalia, CA 93291**

DEDICATED TO MY PARENTS,
FRANK AND G.A.

Special thanks to the following for their inspiration, encouragement and professional know-how: Guy Qvistgaard, Kevin Fitzpatrick, Julia Jane Ritzo, Tia and Ritch Lewis, Lynette Domicq, Ted Hansen, Dan Brown, Mike Gosney, Dave Pique, Shirlee Vitas, Dave Ewing, Myra Sleicher, Mary Crabtree, Dewey and Sylvester Bowen, the folks at Music Sales, the girls at Advance, and the thousands of harmonica players who have written me over the past five years. It wouldn't be possible without you.

In Memoriam: Gerald Landgarten, Dorothy Scott and Bea Erickson. You live on in our hearts.

Introduction

The lights are low as you step to the microphone. In the audience you see faces, the faces of people who have come to hear the hottest band in town – with *you* playing harmonica.

The lights brighten and dim. This means it's time to start. "One-two-three-four!" shouts the drummer. His sticks bang on the drumheads in a frenzy of rhythm. The guitarist strums his opening chord and the bass player dances across the stage, the *boom, boom, boom* of his instrument providing a low-toned support.

The music has started; a churning brew of rhythm and sound that moves people to their feet and out to the dance floor. Now it's your turn. You place your harmonica to your puckered lips. You blow, you draw, you warble and wail. Notes shoot through space, tumbling one after the other, curving and burning through the music.

The audience breaks into applause. This is the sound they've come to hear; the sound of your harmonica accompanying electric guitar, drums and bass. It's the sound of emotion and skill, creativity and fun. It's the sound of today's music. And man, there's nothing else like it.

Rock n' Blues Harmonica is about this sound and the experience of creating it. The book works like this. In Chapter I, you'll read how Adam and Eve discovered notes, scales, chords and chord progressions in the Garden of Eden. While you don't need to memorize this information to play harmonica, getting the basic idea will give you a strong sense of how music is organized. And *this* will help you make music on any instrument, both solo and with a band.

Harmonica instruction begins with Chapter II. You'll meet the world's first rock and blues band, the Cave Boys, and take lessons from their harmonica player, Stone. With Stone's help, you'll learn what kind of harmonica to buy, how to make your first sounds, how to play chords, chord progressions, single notes, blues riffs, how to play with a band, how to play solo, how to bend notes, how to play melodies, how to play in three different harp styles (Cross Harp, Straight Harp and Slant Harp), how to improvise and much more.

Lastly, the back of the book offers a Record Index listing the key of harmonica you need to jam with each song on almost 100 popular record albums. Simply put a record on the turntable, pull out the right key of harmonica, and start playing along. From the music of J. Geils to that of Willie Nelson or Bruce Springsteen, you'll find there's a place for rock n' blues harmonica played in your style. Even if you've never made music before, you'll be amazed how easy it is, and how good it sounds.

So pull out your harmonica (Chapter II tells you what kind) and start making some passionate noises. You've got the music in you. Let *Rock n' Blues Harmonica* help bring it out.

Table of Contents

The Night Music was Discovered
(Theory for Beginners)

It was a magical night. The stars were twinkling and everything was new – including music. This was the night Adam and Eve discovered the note, the chord, and the chord progression. It was the night music was born.

Eight Little Sounds

As everyone knows, music was discovered by Adam and Eve in the Garden of Eden.

Here's how it happened.

One morning Adam was thirsty. He'd been running around the Garden discovering things and giving them names. Cottonmouth (which he'd not yet named) was driving him crazy. So he asked Eve to bring him a glass of iced tea.

Now Eve was a flaxen haired beauty with great legs and a terrific sense of humor. She was also very intelligent. She filled a glass with tea and ice and handed it to Adam. As he took it from her hand, the spoon accidentally struck the glass.

What happened next was incredible. It was a *noise*, a high-pitched ringing tone. Eve's sensitive eardrums could feel this noise vibrating.

"What's that?" Eve asked.

Adam, of course, knew everything. And what he didn't know, he made up. Still, he had no idea what that sound was.

"A..." he began.

"A what?" demanded Eve.

"A...a...it's an **A**," he said, and drank a little more of the tasty tea. As if by miracle, the spoon struck the glass once again.

The glass, being emptier by one swallow, made a tone that was one swallow higher.

"And what's that?" Eve asked.

"Do I have to tell you everything?" snapped Adam. "It's a **B**!" He gave Eve a smarter-than-thou look and sipped again from the glass.

"Typical male," Eve said. But the lady was getting curious. She tapped on the glass with the spoon. Being a little emptier than before, the resulting tone was a little higher.

"And I suppose that's a **C**," Eve said.

"You got it," muttered Adam. He took another swallow. "Tingggg!" sang the glass as Eve struck it with the spoon.

"For crimany sakes, woman," Adam growled. But they both knew that what had occurred was a **D**.

And so it went. Adam drank. Eve played an **E**. Adam sipped once more. Eve clanged a one-beat boogie on an **F**. Again Adam sipped. The new tone was dubbed **G**.

"Big deal," Adam said. He took another swallow. He had now drunk half the iced tea that was originally in the glass. Eve struck the glass with the spoon.

A sound occurred.

"Boy, that sounds familiar," said Eve.

"Of course,"Adam said. "It's the same note we played in the beginning." The highly caffeinated iced tea was beginning to have an effect on him.

"It's an **A**, but a higher **A** than we played when the glass was full. What we've done is play a ladder of sounds starting from **A**." And in his rich tenor voice Adam started to sing:

"A B C D E F G A!"

"You see, Eve, when the glass was full, and the spoon hit it, vibrations came out of the glass into the air. You may not believe this, but I counted 440 vibrations per second. That was the **A** sound.

"Now, I drank a little bit more and you banged the glass again. Since the glass was a bit emptier, the vibration into the air (and our eardrums) was faster. In fact, it was right around 510 vibrations per second. That's the sound we called a **B**."

"I get it," Eve said. "Each time you made the glass a little emptier, the vibrations it made were a little faster, and the resulting tone was higher. But why is the high **A** the same as the low **A**?"

"Don't you see?" Adam said. "The glass vibrated twice as fast, and that makes the sound twice as high."

"I suppose you think that makes you twice as smart," Eve said with a giggle.

"Of course," laughed Adam. "Now let's assign some names to all this. We'll call each sound a NOTE. That gives us an **A** note, a **B** note, a **C** note, and so forth.

"And each ladder of sounds that goes from **A** to **A**, or from **B** to **B** is a SCALE. If you start on an **A**, you have an **A** scale. If you start on a **C**, it's a **C** scale. Not bad, eh?"

"How come you have to name everything?" Eve asked. "Some strange psychological compulsion?"

"And the distance between a high **A** and the low **A**...we'll call that an OCTAVE."

"Call it what you want," Eve said. "Just answer me this. What's it good for?"

"Get me eight glasses of iced tea and we'll find out," Adam said.

Sweet Harmony

That evening, strange sounds were heard in the Garden. There was laughter. Then came a new way of talking that rose and fell in the ·craziest ways. And then, even weirder, came a succession of high-pitched, ringing sounds. *Bong! Clang! Boing!*

It was Adam and Eve, sitting in the glow of the fire, pleasantly blasted on bongo juice, surrounded by glasses, each filled with a different amount of iced tea. Adam was beating his hands on his haunches and snapping his fingers, giving Eve a rhythm in which to explore the tones of the glasses.

"Yeah, yeah," Adam sang. "Yeah, yeah."

"Hey!" cried Eve. "Listen to this!" She was holding a spoon in each hand. "If I strike a **C** note at the same time that I strike an **E**, dig it: the sounds combine."

Firelight flickering on her face, Eve clanged the spoons on the glass filled to **C** and on the glass filled to **E** at the same time.

The two tones collaborated and faded into the night.

"That was beautiful," Adam said. "Do it again."

Once again, Eve struck the **C** and **E** glasses at the same time. The vibrations intertwined to form something rich and sweet.

"What *was* that?" asked a delighted Eve.

"Think I'll call that a...a...a HARMONY," said Adam. "Yes, a harmony is when two notes played at the same time blend together to form a new, combined sound."

"Fair enough," said Eve. "But what happens if I strike the **C** and **D** glasses at the same time?"

To answer her own question, Eve banged her spoons on the two glasses.

Although the **C** and **D** did not clash, neither did they form the beautiful blend that came from the **C** and **E**. Eve frowned. What was going on here?

"I get it!" she suddenly cried. "The **C** and **E** notes are the first and third notes of the **C** scale. **C** is number 1, **D** is number 2, **E** is number 3, and so on.

"If you want a nice blending harmony using the **C**, you strike the 1st and 3rd notes of the **C** scale at the same time.

"And if you want this blend to use the **G** sound, you strike the 1st and 3rd notes of the **G** scale."

To prove her point, Eve struck her spoons on the **G** and **B** glasses. The two sounds combined beautifully.

"See?" cried Eve. "If I play the 1st and 3rd notes of this simple scale at the same time, they merge together. I've got an idea. Let's call the 1st and 3rd notes HARMONIZING NOTES!"

Suddenly, Eve realized her mistake. It was Adam's job to name things. She could discover, but *he* had to name. She looked at him nervously. Would he be angry?

Adam only smiled. Eve looked beautiful with firelight rippling across her long, flowing hair. "Yeah," Adam said, a crazy grin on his face. "The 1st and 3rd notes come together and harmonize when played at the same time. Just like us, baby."

The Incredible Chord

And so the night went. Much bongo juice was consumed. The laughing, the strange way of talking, the piercing sounds of glasses struck with spoons...it was all so new. Even The Landlord stopped to cock His head and listen.

Meanwhile, the couple in the Garden were making important discoveries about this thing called music. They learned that not only did the 1st and 3rd notes of each scale come together and harmonize when played at the same time – but that the 5th note of the scale also harmonized.

Adam called this combination of three harmonizing notes played at the same time a CHORD. To play a **C** chord, Eve would strike the glasses that produced a **C** note and an **E** note, the 1st and 3rd notes of the **C** scale. At exactly the same time, Adam would bang on the 5th note of the scale – the **G** note.

The **C, E,** and **G** notes flowed into each other and produced what Adam called a **C** chord.

Then, Eve struck the 1st, 3rd and 5th notes of the **G** scale. **G** was the 1st note, **B** was the 3rd note and **D** was the 5th note. This produced the **G** chord.

another major chord

G 1   B 3   D 5

"Hey!" shouted Adam. I think we're on to something!"

Without thinking what he was doing, he picked up the 6th glass of the **C** scale and started to drink. He had half a swallow in his mouth when Eve squealed, "What are you doing?"

Coughing, half-choking, face red with embarrassment, Adam put the glass back in its number 6 spot. "I thought it was bongo juice," he started to say, but stopped himself.

"I know *exactly* what I'm doing," he said imperiously.

"And what *exactly* is that?" demanded Eve.

"I wanted to see what would happen if I made the 6th note a little higher by making the glass half a swallow emptier. Know what I mean? Now the glass is halfway between the 6th and 7th note of the **C** scale. It's a 6½ glass."

"Real sharp, flathead!" shouted Eve.

But Adam knew the best discoveries often occurred by mistake. "Let's see what happens when you play the 1st, 3rd and 5th notes of **C** scale at the same time that I bang on the 6½ note."

"Whatever you say," answered Eve. She banged her spoons on the 1st, 3rd and 5th glasses while Adam played his 6½ glass.

the bluesy 7th chord

What a sound! It was odd, yet powerful, speaking of the ironies of a life filled with passions and disappointments, new loves and sad goodbyes. All this was pretty heady stuff for Adam who had spent all his young life in the Garden of Eden. Still, he must have had a sense of what was to come.

"This chord, this combination of 1st, 3rd, 5th and 6½ notes of a scale shall henceforth be called a 7th CHORD (in this case C7th)."

He looked triumphantly at Eve and wobbled a little. "And the 7th chord shall be the mainstay, the distinguishing characteristic of the type of music that will someday be called THE BLUES."

At that, Eve grabbed Adam and laughingly pulled him to the ground, covering him with kisses. "I'll give you the blues," she murmered, pulling him closer.

---

* The term **B** flat refers to the note halfway between the **A** and the **B**. This note could also be called **A** sharp, but rarely is. Including sharps and flats (also known as halfsteps), there are 12 notes in a scale: **A** flat, **A, B** flat, **B, C, C** sharp, **D, E** flat, **E, F, F**sharp, **G**.

Majors and Minors

Well, they played and played. All of it in the key of **C**, of course.

KEY? That's the word Adam used to identify the idea that in music, if you start a song on a **C** note, you usually end the song on a **C** note. Thus you're playing in the key of **C**.

In the same vein, when you start a song on an **E** note, you usually end the song on the **E** note – and are playing in the key of **E**.

At any rate, as Adam and Eve arranged and rearranged glasses and struck them with spoons, they learned a few things about music that would intrigue musicians for years to come.

1. Woman likes to boogie as much as man.

2. Clinking spoons on glasses of iced tea is a hell of a way to make music.

3. When playing in the key of **C**, you can play the basic chord, the major chord, by striking the 1st, 3rd and 5th glasses of the scale.

4. You can get a blues sound by including the 6½ note with the 1st, 3rd and 5th.

5. You can get a mysterious, eerie sounding chord by playing the 1st, 2½ and 5th glasses of a scale. Adam called this a MINOR CHORD.

6. And, playing the 1st, 3rd, 5th and 6th produces a jazzy sounding chord. This was called a MAJOR 6th.

In fact, the list of chords Adam and Eve discovered that evening was endless. There were no limits on the tones these notes could combine to form.

As Eve went from one chord to the next, it was easy to imagine her the precursor of today's electric guitarist. She shook her head and her long hair swished back over her shoulder. She lifted her spoon-holding hands and brought them down in a wide arc, almost as though she were strumming the glasses.

"Yeah, yeah," Adam sang. Although he didn't know it, his girlfriend Eve was on the verge of a new discovery – a discovery that would create the chord framework for the types of music that would one day be known as country western, blues, punk, disco, reggae, folk, rock a' billy, gospel, tex-mex, schlock and rock and roll.

This discovery was the I-IV-V CHORD PROGRESSION. Here's how it happened.

The I-IV-V of Music

Eve arranged the iced-tea glasses into rows of major chords.

First, she bonged the **C** chord 4 times in a row. Then she clanged on the **F** chord, the chord 4 glasses up the scale from the **C**.

She played these two chords over and over and it sounded terrific. Four beats on the I chord, four beats on the IV chord. This was the birth of the TWO-CHORD JAM.

But there was much more to learn. This was when Eve discovered she could add to the two-chord feeling by bonging the **G** chord, the chord 5 glasses up the scale from the **C** chord.

This V chord (the **G** chord when played in the key of **C**) took the music further away from the I chord. It added a sense of transition, a feeling of drama and *tension*.

It sounded great to pound out a beat on the I chord, then the IV chord, then back to the I chord. Now was the time to play the V chord, slip down to the IV chord, and with an air of finality and resolution, return to the I chord.

Wow! This I-IV-V progression really made sense. It put the sounds into a cycle, gave them a beginning and an end. It created and resolved tension. It organized sound to tell a story.

Even Adam was amazed as Eve hunched over her rows of iced tea glasses and played these beautiful sequences of harmonizing notes. He *had* to jam. But how? How does one musician accompany another? Spoon in hand, the original man set out to make a new discovery.

Accompanying the I-IV-V Chord Progression

Adam knew Eve was playing her I-IV-V chord progression in the key of **C**. Following a hunch, he started banging on his **C** glass. It sounded pretty good! While Eve went from one chord to the next, all Adam had to do was play the 1st note of the scale.

But Eve, swinging spoons like a maestro, wanted more. "C'mon!" she shouted over the loud clinking of iced tea glasses. "Get it on!"

So get it on is exactly what Adam did. But he paid attention,too. Soon he realized that certain iced tea glasses sounded great no matter where the music was in the I-IV-V progression.

The glasses that always sounded so great were none other than the 1st, 3rd and 5th notes of the **C** scale. These were the harmonizing notes that made up the **C** chord.

By accenting these harmonizing notes (playing them longer and playing them louder), and using other notes in the **C** scale as stepping stones between one harmonizing note and another, Adam created melodic patterns that swirled confidently through Eve's I-IV-V progression of chords.

Amazingly, it didn't matter when Adam hit the 1st, 3rd or 5th note. Each would work at any point in the chord progression.

Now Adam decided to get fancy. He started banging on the 2½ glass, the glass which was left over from the minor chord. What a sound! Sexy, sultry, bluesy. He banged the 2½ glass again, and *again*. Like the 1st, 3rd and 5th notes, it worked through all of Eve's chord changes.

But this 2½ note did more than simply accompany the I-IV-V chord progression. Somehow, it changed the music, made it hard. Made it tense. Made it bluesy.

It was a BLUES HARMONIZING NOTE.

2½

"Alright!" shouted Eve. As the original blues lady bonged a steady beat on the I-IV-V progression, Adam explored every nook and cranny of the **C** scale. He banged the 1st note six or seven times (it didn't matter). Then he clanged the 5th note, the 4th note, the 2½ note, and finally returned to the 1st note.

Then he was off again, at one time or another striking a spoon on every glass he could see. Some glasses sounded terrible, and some sounded like they were born to make music. Finally, through trial and error, Adam discovered the BLUES SCALE.

Starting with the **C** note and going up the scale, the blues scale went: 1   2½   4   5   6½   1.*

What a sound this blues scale created! What a feeling! Eve, by now, was playing progressive jazz chords, using minors, major sixths, altering the chord progression in innumerable ways, playing rock, reggae, blues and country western, yet never leaving the key of **C**. Adam, too, was swept away by the ringing tones of iced tea glasses. Eve could play any chord she wanted, and as long as she always returned to her **C** chord, her I chord, Adam's wonderful new blues scale would not make a mistake.

This was the kind of music that could go on forever. (And in a way, it has.) But even the original man and woman occasionally got tired.

As the sun rose in the eastern sky and the light of a new day shone on the young, musical world, Adam yawned. Eve yawned. The tight rhythms of Eve's chord progression and Adam's accompaniment took slack. Mistakes were made, but neither musician cared.

Finally, the music stopped altogether. The Landlord took a deep breath as Adam and Eve crawled into the trees and fell asleep in each others arms.

~~~

Adam and Eve awakened with hangovers the following afternoon. A few days later they were asked to leave the Garden for good. It seems Adam had hooked up iced tea glasses to amplifiers and had been playing them at outrageous volumes.

On her way out of the Garden into the Wilderness, Eve picked a piece of bark off a tree, a tree Adam had previously named the boo boo tree. She chewed on the sweet bark as she walked. Then, before she knew it, she was holding the reed-like thing between her teeth and blowing and drawing.

What a strange sounds that piece of vibrating bark made! It was almost like a duck. *Wa Wo Wa!*

Adam turned to Eve. "What's that?" he asked. "What are those sounds?"

Eve only smiled.

Notes

* The NOTE is the basic unit of music.

* Notes form SCALES. If the first note of the scale is a **C**, this is a **C** scale. If the first note is a **G**, it's a **G** scale.

* When played at the same time, the 1st, 3rd and 5th notes of a scale HARMONIZE to form a MAJOR CHORD. The 1st, 3rd and 5th notes of a **C** scale play a **C** major chord. Likewise for an **A** or a **B** scale.

* The structure of most rock, blues and country western music is built around the I-IV-V CHORD PROGRESSION.

* Moving from one chord to the next forms a CYCLE. The I chord is the HOME BASE, the place where the music usually starts and ends. The IV chord moves the music further away from home base. The V chord moves it further still. Being away from home creates MUSICAL TENSION. Returning home RESOLVES THE TENSION.

*There are many VARIATIONS to the above cycle, but the I-IV-V progression is the foundation on which they're based.

* A simple way to ACCOMPANY another instrument playing the I-IV-V chord progression (or a variation) is to play musical patterns that emphasize the 1st, 3rd and 5th notes of the I chord's scale. No matter what chord the music plays, these HARMONIZING NOTES will not make a mistake.

* This accompaniment can sound BLUESY by including the 2½ note of the I chord's major scale.

* If this leaves you slightly confused, don't worry. Many harmonica players know much less than you about the structure of music and play just great!

TWO

First Sounds of the Harmonica

Now that you have an idea how music is organized, it's time to pull out your harmonica and start making your own sounds. In Chapter II, you'll meet the world's first rock band, The Cave Boys, their harp player, Stone, and you will learn the harmonica essentials – what kind of harp to play, how to make your first sounds, and how to play chords and single notes.

Legend of the Cave Boys

From what little we know, the world's first rock band was a four person group called the Cave Boys. They played drums, bass, guitar and harmonica – amplifying their instruments through valuable electric tree stumps for which they had scoured the countryside.

The legend also tells us of Umm, the beautiful female vocalist who joined the Cave Boys and led them to stardom with such prehistoric hits as "Tango in the Tarpits" and "Funky Dinosaur."

The story that hasn't yet been told is that of Stone, the band's harmonica player. He started as a boy on a hillside with only the crickets and the coyotes for accompaniment. He went on to make the sweetest blues and rock harmonica sounds the world has ever heard.

What were Stone's secrets? How was he able to make that harmonica bend and warble with so much feeling – and always in perfect accompaniment to the band's pounding I-IV-V chord progression? How was he able to play bluesy sounding Cross Harp, then melodic Straight Harp, and finally exotic, minor key Slant Harp? Was he a human being or some bizarre musical god?

This story now belongs to you. All you need is a harmonica, a pair of lips, and a sense of fun. Dig it. Stone didn't know a lot about music, but he knew how to play it. As you're about to discover, you can play it too.

What Kind of Harmonica?

To play blues, rock, folk or country western harp, you need a
10 HOLED DIATONIC HARMONICA.

This is the standard, small harmonica (about 4 inches long) that was
originally designed and manufactured by the M. Hohner Company
back in the 1800's.

Today, the best diatonic harps cost about $11.00 and probably
produce more music per dollar than any other instrument you can
name.

Hohner makes eleven different models of diatonic harmonicas.
Those used by most harp players (and recommended for you) are:

1. GOLDEN MELODY – fits well in your hand (especially with a
microphone), responds easily in the high range, has plastic stops.
However, if you're going to play guitar and harmonica at the same
time, the Golden Melody does not fit snugly in a harmonica rack.

2. SPECIAL 20 – a smooth sounding, airtight instrument with excep-
tional tone and ease in playing. It *does* fit smoothly in a harmonica
rack. The author plays the Special 20 harp.

3. THE MARINE BAND – the original diatonic harp and favorite of
many. This harp fits snugly in a harmonica rack but its wooden frame
sometimes swells from moisture.

4. BLUES HARP – designed by Hohner's specialists especially for
blues players. Reeds are set higher for easier bending and greater
durability.

Other types of diatonic harmonicas include: American Ace, Old
Standby, Pocket Pal, Vest Pocket Harp, Scout, Lancer, and
Orchestra I. If they are in good condition, each of these harps will
work for playing blues, rock, country and folk harmonica.

Diatonic harmonicas come in each of music's twelve different keys.
If this is your first harmonica, the key of **C** is recommended.
If you already own a **C** harp, other versatile keys are **A, D, F** and
G. G is the lowest toned harmonica you can buy. **F** sharp is the
highest.

A Closer Look

Stone's harmonicas were carefully carved from the tusk of wild boar with reeds fashioned from the hard bark of the boo boo tree. There are only a few of these harps in existence today. Of course, they're priceless.

The rest of us play harmonicas with nickle plated covers, wood or plastic air chambers, and brass reeds.

From 1 through 10, each air chamber (or hole) is numbered. Inside each air chamber are two reeds: thin strips of metal of different lengths. The reed on the ceiling of the air chamber vibrates when air is BLOWN through the harmonica. The reed on the floor of the chamber responds when air is sucked or DRAWN through the harp.

Thus, each hole has a blow note and a draw note.

On holes 1 through 6, blow notes are lower than draw notes. The situation reverses itself on holes 7 through 10. Up here draw notes are lower than blow notes.

When this book refers to, say, 4 draw, it means suck on hole 4. Four blow, or *4 blow*, means to blow on hole 4. In the charts and graphs, the number 4 with a circle around it means 4 draw. An uncircled 4 means 4 blow.

Here are some additional facts about your harmonica:

* The key of your harp is etched on its right end. If you own a **C** harp, 1 blow plays a **C** note. On a **D** harp, 1 blow is a **D** note.

* When playing, the key of your harmonica and the numbers identifying each hole should be facing up.

* The only complete scale on your harmonica goes from 4 blow through 7 blow. Holes 1 through 4 and 7 through 10 have "missing notes."

Lay Out of Notes on C Harp

* Almost all the notes on your harp can be expressed in octaves. For instance, 1 draw is the same note as 4 draw and 8 draw. They are simply an octave apart. One blow is the same note as 4 blow and 7 blow. Three blow is the same note as 6 blow and 9 blow.

* From **G** (your lowest harp) through **F** sharp (your highest harmonica), the 12 different keyed harmonicas are organized exactly the same. If, by playing 6 blow, 5 draw, 4 draw, 4 blow, 3 draw, 3 blow, you can play a blues scale on your **G** harp, this same pattern of blows and draws will play a blues scale on your **F** sharp harmonica.

The only difference is that your **G** harp's blues scale will be very low in tone, and the blues scale on your **F** sharp harmonica will be quite high. This is the PRINCIPLE OF HARMONICA RELATIVITY: although they play in different keys, all harps have the same relationships of notes, scales and chords.

The Principle of Harmonica Relativity is both a convenience and a hassle. The hassle is that you need to carry around a number of different key harmonicas, and you never seem to have the one you need. The convenience is that you only have to learn a blues riff (pattern of notes) once to play it all different keys.

First Sounds

Even Stone had to start somewhere.

The first sounds he made on his harmonica were rough and uncontrolled. "Will you shut up?" his father would yell as the young harp player sat in the corner of the cave and practiced. "You're going to attract dinosaurs!"

Amazingly, no dinosaurs came. And, as Stone became more familiar with his harp – the feel of it in his mouth, the sensation of sounds produced by blowing and drawing, changing the sounds by changing the shape of his lips and mouth – his music became admired instead of scorned.

Now it's your turn. Numbers facing up, put your harmonica to your lips. Make your mouth big enough to cover holes 1, 2, 3 and 4 at the same time. You may want to stretch a finger across holes 5, 6, 7, 8, 9 and 10 so you know where holes 1, 2, 3 and 4 are.

Keeping your mouth relaxed, blow gently into holes 1, 2, 3 and 4. Excellent! You've just played a major chord, the combination of 1-3-5 harmonizing notes that were discovered by Adam and Eve.

To play another major chord, draw on holes 1, 2, 3, 4. Listen as you play. This draw chord is higher than the blow chord. By going back and forth between the draw chord and the blow chord, you can play a simple two chord harmonica jam.

After you've explored the blows and draws of holes 1, 2, 3 and 4, slide the harp up one hole so you're playing 2, 3, 4 and 5. Blow and draw and move the harp up another hole to 3, 4, 5 and 6. Blow and draw. Listen to the sounds of your harmonica. Make your breathing gentle and controlled as you slide the harp from one end to the other.

Some tips on moving the harmonica and playing chords:

1. Move the harp, not your head.

2. To make sure you're including hole number 1, place the low end of your harp in the corners of your lips.

3. If your chords have a bleating, forced quality, your mouth is too tight on the harp. Relax. Don't force the sounds. Clenching the harmonica between your teeth and blowing and drawing will give you an idea of how rich and full these chords can sound.

4. When blowing, let air escape over the top of your harp. This will improve your tone, keep you from running out of breath, and lighten the air pressure on the reeds.

With these suggestions in mind, continue exploring the sounds of your harmonica. Make your playing slow and lazy. Learn to relax when the harmonica is in your mouth.

Stomping

As you blow and draw your way up and down your harmonica, begin stomping a beat on the floor. Make this beat slow and steady. Count "1 – 2 – 1 – 2" or "1 – 2 – 3 – 4 – 1 – 2 – 3 – 4." Playing to a beat will give meaning and feeling to the sounds you make on your harp. Remember: rhythm is at least half of music.

You can also get a beat by listening to the mechanical hum of a washing machine, the clicking and slurping of windshield wipers, the dripping of a faucet, or the busy signal on a telephone. Metronomes, drum machines, drum records and even real live drummers have been known to work. The important thing is to play to a beat.

Tonguing

Make a long blow or draw sound on your harp. Now flick the tip of your tongue – as though you were saying *ta ta ta* – on the ridge behind your upper teeth.

This *ta ta ta* tonguing action will stop and start the air traveling through your harp. This will stop and start the sound of your harp. The result is total control of a crisp, rhythmic harp sound. Now you can play your blows and draws for four, eight, or sixteen beats each, and by tonguing quickly, make the harp sound as though you were playing fast enough to beat the devil.

But *fast* is not the only form of rhythm. Making some sounds long and others short as in *taaaaa ta* or *tata taaaaa taaaaaa* is also very effective.

Spend a few minutes using your tongue to put rhythm into your impromptu harp music. DO NOT stop your breath when you tongue. Keep the air flow moving and let your tongue play the percussion.

Train Jam

Although Stone never saw a train, he played train music like nobody's business. The harp sounds like a train when it huffs and puffs, builds up speed, goes faster and faster, and then, with the next station in view, slowly comes to a halt.

You can play train music (sometimes called Freight Harp) by going back and forth between the 1234 draw chord and the 1234 blow chord, giving each chord 1 beat. This is a I to IV chord jam.

(1234) 1234 (1234) 1234 (1234)
Draw Blow Draw Blow Draw
I IV I IV I

Start slowly, like a train leaving the station. Draw. Blow. Draw. Blow. Gradually go faster, letting air escape over the top of your harp on the blow chords.

Once your train is chugging down the track, you may want to try making a whistle sound. Draw holes 45 for eight beats, making these two notes cry out like the whistle of a train.

(45)
Waaaaaaaaaaaaaaaaaaaaaaaaah!
V

Without hesitating, return to your 1234 draw and blow pattern, playing the draw chord *before* you blow. Now, begin slowing down, like a train that knows the station is only a mile away.

Slower still, Chugalug, chugalug, chugalug on your 1234 draw and 1234 blow.

And finally, bring your train into the station, home at last.

(45)
Waaaaaaaaaaaaaaaaaaaaaaaah!

The I-IV-V of Harmonica

Since the earliest times, the I-IV-V chord progression or blues cycle has served as the framework for popular music. Adam and Eve used it. Stone used it. Now it's your turn.

When playing the style of harmonica known as Cross Harp (see the next chapter), your I chord is played by drawing on holes 1, 2, 3 and 4. Because the I chord is where the music usually starts and ends, it's called the CHORD OF RESOLUTION.

I Cross Harp Chord of Resolution
1234 Draw

The IV chord can be played by blowing on holes 1, 2, 3 and 4. The IV chord moves the music away from the Chord of Resolution. It's called the STEPPING STONE CHORD.

IV Cross Harp Stepping Stone Chord
1234 Blow

The V chord can be played by drawing on holes 4 and 5. The V chord creates musical tension, and is called the DOMINANT WAILER CHORD.

V   Cross Harp Dominant Wailer Chord
45 Draw

To play a simple I-IV-V chord progression, begin stomping your foot 1-2-1-2.* Once you've got a beat going, play the Cross Harp Chord of Resolution for two stomps. Play the Stepping Stone Chord for two stomps. Play the Dominant Wailer Chord for two stomps. Complete your blues cycle by returning to the Chord of Resolution. Then play the cycle again.

---

* How fast should you stomp? Try pulse speed. Place your thumb on the big vein of your wrist. Feel the rhythm of your heartbeat. The first beat is 1, the second is 2, the third is 1 and so on. Start stomping at the same speed.

I-IV-V Beginner's Cycle

| (1234) Resolution I | 1234 Stepping IV | (45) Wailing V | (1234) Resolution I |

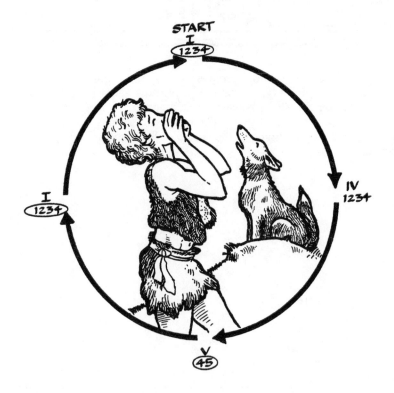

You can add rhythm and meaning by tonguing every chord twice.

You can change the order of chords in a I-IV-V progression. The next chord cycle plays the Dominant Wailer V Chord BEFORE the Stepping Stone IV Chord.

Foot Stomper's Cycle

(1234) Resolution I　　(45) Wailing V　　1234 Stepping IV　　(1234) Resolution I

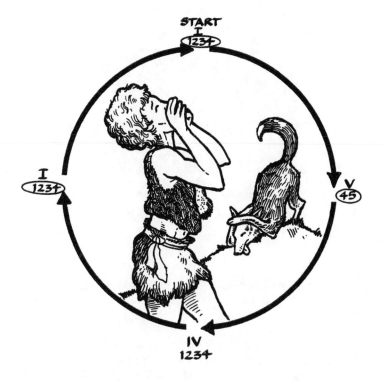

START
I
1234

I
1234

V
45

IV
1234

After you've played the above chord cycle a few times without tonguing, tongue every chord three times each time you bring your foot down (this is called a triplet). Not tonguing the final Chord of Resolution will add to the sense of completion.

The next chord cycle starts on the Dominant Wailer and ends on the Chord of Resolution.

Dancing Dog Cycle

(45)   (1234)   1234   (1234)
Wailer   Resolution   Stepping   Resolution
  V   I   IV   I

START
V
(45)

I
(1234)

I
(1234)

IV
1234

A suggestion for putting rhythm in the above cycle is to tongue every chord twice. Tonguing the final Chord of Resolution three times will add still more pzazzz.

Get a rhythm going and play these chords over and over. Stomp your foot 1-2-1-2-1-2. Play harp as you march around the house. Clap your hands as you clench your harp in your teeth. Do anything that will help you return to that ancient cave of your mind and that subterranean river where music and rhythm flow.

In other words, get it on!

46

The Sensuous Single Note

Although Stone was a rough and tumble Cave Boy, he had his sensuous side. But Stone had a problem. He couldn't run around being sensuous with everybody he met; he'd be arrested. So Stone learned to convey his sensuality through the harmonica.

This sensuous approach was most important when playing a single note: playing one note at a time. It was as though he treated the harmonica as a person, a person he cared about. The result was a rich, clear single note that would do anything he asked it to.

Now it's your turn to play a single note. Before you sits your harmonica. "Play me," it says, "Pick me up and play a sweet single note."

Being the obedient type (especially when it comes to your harmonica) you place your little friend to your puckered lips. You blow through hole number 3, and play a clear single note.

"Ahhhh..." moans your harmonica. "It feels so good when you massage my reeds. And I love the way you pucker."

Indeed. Your lips are pushed out, well over the silver plates of your harmonica. Your tongue rests on the bottom of your mouth. Your airstream is gentle but persuasive as it guides a sweet 3 blow out of the harp and into the atmosphere.

"Play the Beginner's Blues Riff," says the harp. "You can do it."

Slowly, you move the harmonica about a quarter inch to the right and DRAW on hole 4.

"Yes!"cries the harp. "Four draw. But I do need a feeling of musical tension. Tongue me. Please."

As you draw on hole 4, you tap the tip of your tongue on the fleshy ridge behind your upper teeth. *Ta ta ta. Ta ta ta.* The flicking tip of your tongue punctuates the wailing 4 draw. Musical tension builds as this important blues harmonica note belts out phrases the same way a singer belts out words.

④
"My baby left me this morning!"
Ta   tata   ta   ta   ta

You swivel your harp from the 4 draw back to the 3 blow. Your tongue taps out the singer's phrasing of:

3
"I don't know what to do!"
Ta   ta   ta   ta   ta ta

The voice of your harp is pure and rich. The punctuation of your tongue gives meaning and feeling to the 3 blow and the 4 draw.

And your harp? "Mmmmmmmmm" it says, "you sure know how to play single notes. Especially for someone just starting out."

○ means draw

The Practical Single Note

Decide which note you want to play, line it up to your puckered lips, and kiss that harp. The trick is in the pucker. Push your lips out so they form a vertical oval – a tongue moistened gateway that's higher than it is wide. Now, PLAY THAT NOTE.

Some tips:

1. Practice your single notes for 8, 12 or 16 beats so you have a chance to hear and improve them.

2. Don't hold your harp on the edges of your lips. The further in your mouth you can put your harp, the richer will be your tone.

3. Don't press your upper lip down on the harp. Don't make it stretch or reach for the harp. Move the harp and your puckered mouthpiece *up* towards your nose. Rest your upper lip on the top plate of the harp.

4. Make your single note hole as big as possible. Make your lips big and flabby feeling. Don't puff out your cheeks.

5. Blow and draw smooth, round airstreams from and to top of your throat and nasal passages. This is called playing from your head. Do everything gently and smoothly. Play softly, but firmly. Control your air.

6. Think of an air tunnel that starts where your lips pucker around the harp and goes to the top of your head and down into your voice box and stomach. Let the air flow freely through this tunnel.

7. Give the airstream a start and stop stutter effect by tonguing.

8. If you start to hear part of another note along with your single note, pucker more.

9. If you have trouble finding the note you want, mark it with a piece of tape on your harmonica.

10. When searching for a note, don't pull your harp out of your mouth. Rather, slide the harp sideways between your moistened lips. Continue blowing or drawing as you slide.

11. Be patient. Listen to your single note. The more you relax, the better it will sound. Clear single notes are the keys to good harp playing.

Final Words for Chapter Two

By now you should be exploring the sounds of your harmonica with great fervor. Some of these noises will sound great; others terrible. The important thing is to feel relaxed with your harmonica, to not try *too* hard.

Continue blowing and drawing as you read through Chapters II, III, IV, V and beyond. Soon your chords, single notes, and ability to play to a beat will come into their own.

Until then, be patient, spontaneous, and most important, have fun.

Notes

* To play blues, rock or country harmonica, you need a small, ten-holed diatonic harmonica.

* The most frequently used keys are **A, C, D, F** and **G**.

* The different keyed harmonicas are organized exactly the same. If you can play a song or "riff" on a **C** harp, you can play the same song on any other key of harmonica. This is the PRINCIPLE OF HARMONICA RELATIVITY.

* Make the first sounds on your harmonica relaxed and easy.

* Put RHYTHM into your sounds by TONGUING, tapping the tip of your tongue behind your upper teeth as in *ta ta ta*.

* Throughout this book, a circled number means DRAW. An uncircled number means BLOW.

* To play a I-IV-V CHORD PROGRESSION, make 1234 draw your I chord, 1234 blow your IV chord, and play your V chord by drawing on holes 4 and 5. Be sure to resolve on 1234 draw.

* Playing clear SINGLE NOTES is essential to playing sensuous harmonica. Practice on 3 blow and 4 draw.

THREE

Cross Harp: Sound of the Blues

Cross Harp is the style of harmonica that plays the blues. It involves accenting the draw notes instead of the blow notes and playing a C harmonica in the key of G. Chapter III will introduce you to Cross Harp and get you started making those wailing blues sounds.

Straight Harp: Playing C Harp in the Key of C

One reason Stone became so intimate with his boo boo tree **C** harp was that he could play it anytime, anywhere.

For instance, he could play while taking a bath in the steamy hot pools behind his cave. The sounds he'd make would echo off the rock canyon walls, flowing like water itself. Or, the fledgling cave boy might play while walking along the streets of Cave City, huffing and puffing a draw blow rhythm to some primitive variation of the I-IV-V progression.

From all this playing, Stone discovered two basic harmonica styles: STRAIGHT HARP and CROSS HARP. Straight Harp, which accented the BLOW notes, worked best for playing melodies. Cross Harp, stressing the draw notes, produced a sweet, bluesy sound that created and resolved tension, used Adam's 1-2½-4-5-6½-1 Blues Scale, and made it impossible for people hearing it to feel lonely or out of sorts.

Remembering that music is made up of harmonizing notes and chords (as well as rhythm and soul), here's a good way to understand Straight Harp.

On your **C** harmonica, blowing on holes 1234 at the same time produces a **C** chord. Higher **C** chords can be played by blowing on holes 4567 or 789 and 10. These are the Straight Harp Blow Chords.

Playing your harmonica in a way that accents the 1-3-5 harmonizing notes that make up each of these **C** chords allows you to play your **C** harmonica in the key of **C**. This is Straight Harp.

This is where these Straight Harp harmonizing notes are located.

Straight Harp Harmonizing Notes

Notice that *every* blow note is a harmonizer. Some are the 1st note of the **C** scale. Others are the 3rd or 5th note. And remember: when accompanying a I-IV-V chord progression being played on piano, guitar (or iced tea glasses), the harmonizing notes will always sound good — no matter what phase of the music the chord progression the music is in.

So, to play Straight Harp, accent the BLOW notes. Use the draw non-harmonizing notes as stepping stones between one harmonizer and the next.

Chapter VIII explains Straight Harp in greater detail. Chapter IX presents simple Straight Harp songs you can learn to play. For now, move up and down your harmonica, blowing and drawing, accenting the blows. To accent a note, play it longer, louder and with more feeling.

Finally, end your Straight Harp jam by blowing on holes 1234 or any other Straight Harp Blow Chord. That's how you play a **C** harp in the key of **C**.

---

* No need to memorize this. Just notice that every blow note is a harmonizer.

Cross Harp:
<u>C</u> Harp in the Key of <u>G</u>

Cross Harp is the bluesy, get-down, gutsy, sexy style of harmonica that plays blues, rock and country western. This is the style that the streets of Cave City seemed to bring out of Stone. It's the style that eventually made the Cave Boy harpist famous. Here's how it works:

When you DRAW on holes 1234 of your **C** harp, you play a **G** chord.

Cross Harp Draw Chord

Accenting the harmonizing notes (and the blues harmonizing notes) that make up this Cross Harp Draw Chord is how you play your **C** harmonica in the key of **G**.

This is where the Cross Harp harmonizing notes are located:

Cross Harp Harmonizers

To play primitive Cross Harp, move up and down your harmonica, drawing and blowing, accenting the draws. End your jam on the Cross Harp Draw Chord.

Now that's the blues!

Musical Tension

Stone had a slightly more sophisticated approach to playing Cross Harp. He would create and resolve musical tension. To start, he'd establish home base for the sounds he was going to make. If the music were in the key of **G**, his home base would be a **G** note.

After tonguing out a rhythm on this home base, Stone would blow and draw his way up or down the harmonica to a blues harmonizing note – usually the 2nd, 2½ or 5th notes of Adam's Blues Scale. The harmonizer would sound terrific, but because it was away from home, it created a sense of TENSION. It *wailed*.

Then, when the moment felt right (depending on the timing of the music and the mood he wanted to create), Stone would draw and blow his way back to home base, RESOLVING the tension.

The result would be a feeling that the music had gone somewhere and returned, that the notes of Stone's harmonica had told a story – and that the story had a complete, satisfactory ending.

The notes that resolved the tension, the home base notes, were called NOTES OF RESOLUTION. These notes are 2 draw and 3 blow (which are the same note), 6 blow and 9 blow.

Cross Harp Notes of Resolution
2 Draw, 3 Blow, 6 Blow, 9 Blow

Notes of Resolution are the 1st note of the scale of the key you are playing in. When you play a **C** harp in the key of **G**, your Notes of Resolution are the **G** notes on this **C** harp.

The notes that created tension were called WAILING NOTES. These were the harmonizing notes and blues harmonizing notes of the Cross Harp Draw Chord. They were all played on the draw.

Cross Harp Wailing Notes
1 Draw, 3 Draw, 4 Draw, 6 Draw, 8 Draw

Accompanying a I-IV-V chord progression, Notes of Resolution and Wailing Notes will always harmonize with the music. Be sure you're playing the right key of harmonica and toot along on 3 blow (a Note of Resolution) or 4 draw (a Wailer). Grunt a lot. Wear dark glasses. Your friends will be amazed you've become a harp player so quickly.

If you don't want them to know you've only been playing harp for twenty minutes, avoid accenting the non-harmonizing notes. These non-harmonizers are mostly blow notes and are used as stepping stones between one harmonizer and the next. This is why they are called Stepping Stone Notes.

Stepping Stone Notes will sometimes harmonize when accompanying a I-IV-V chord progression, but not always. On the harmonica below, Cross Harp Wailing Notes and Notes of Resolution are portrayed in black and Stepping Stone Notes expressed in white.

---

* As explained in Chapter VII, 3 draw does not sound bluesy unless it is "bent". Bending is a technique that lets you lower the tone of the note by drawing the air *down* into your voice box. Three draw unbent is the 3rd note of the scale. Three draw bent is Adam's 2½ Blues Harmonizing Note.

Map of Cross Harp

	10	Stepping Stone
	(10)	Stepping Stone
	9	RESOLUTION
	(9)	Stepping Stone
	8	Stepping Stone
	(8)	WAILING
	7	Stepping Stone
	(7)	Stepping Stone
	(6)	WAILING
	6	RESOLUTION
	(5)	Stepping Stone
	5	Stepping Stone
	(4)	WAILING
	4	Stepping Stone
	(3)	WAILING
	3	RESOLUTION
	(2)	RESOLUTION
	2	Stepping Stone
	(1)	WAILING
	1	Stepping Stone

NOTES OF RESOLUTION are home base. They are harmonizers, the 1st note of the scale of the key you're playing in.

WAILING NOTES create musical tension. They are blues harmonizers, the 2nd, 2½, 3rd and 5th notes of the scale.

STEPPING STONE NOTES *don't* always harmonize, though sometimes they sound great. Use them as steps between resolution and tension.

Cross Harp Boogie

Tap out a 3 blow on your harp. Stomp your foot and loosen up. That's right....

Now move that harp a tiny bit and draw on hole 4. Tongue that baby. Create a little tension. Hold that note as you stomp 1-2-1-2-1-2.

Now pause. *Feel* the tension you've created. Dig the silence. Now, and only now, play your Note of Resolution, 3 blow.

Oh yeah! Establish home base. Create tension. Resolve tension. Stomp your foot. Get down. Do it again. Whew! Play a lonnnnnnng 4 draw to the 1-2-1-2 beat.

Now, blow on hole 4, draw on 3 and resolve on 3 blow.

What a sound! *Stress* those harmonizing notes. Glide over those Stepping Stones.

Tongue that 3 blow. Create tension on 3 draw. Resolve on 3 blow. Keep your rhythm going....

Play a long, wailing 6 draw. *Ta ta ta, ta ta ta, ta ta ta.*

Resolve your tension on 6 blow.

Oh yeah! Get down and loosen up! You've got the blues in your shoes. Play 'em.

The Cross Harp Formula

The Cross Harp formula is a simple way to choose the correct key harmonica when playing Cross Harp to accompany a guitarist or piano player.

Ask the guitarist what key the song is in. If the answer is **G**, count up four steps (including the **G**)…

G A B C
1 2 3 4

…and play your **C** harp in the key of **G**.

Likewise, if you have a **C** harp, and want to tell the guitarist what key to play in, count *back* four steps from the **C**. (It's okay to use your fingers!)

G A B C
4 3 2 1

Here is a chart that tells you which harmonica you need to play Cross Harp in each of music's twelve different keys.

Musical Key	Key of Harp for Cross Harp
A flat	D flat
A	D
B flat	E flat
B	E
C	F
D flat	F sharp
D	G
E flat	A flat
E	A
F	B flat
F sharp	B
G	C

HOW TO FIGURE THE CROSS HARP FORMULA.

Notes

* There are two basic styles of harmonica playing: STRAIGHT HARP and CROSS HARP.

* Straight Harp accents the blow notes. When you play your **C** harmonica in the key of **C**, you are playing Straight Harp. Straight Harp works best for melodic harmonica.

* Cross Harp emphasizes the harmonica's draw notes. This blues harmonica style lets you play your **C** harmonica in the key of **G**.

* There are two kinds of notes on your harmonica: HARMONIZING NOTES and STEPPING STONES. Accompanying a I-IV-V chord progression, harmonizing notes will never make a mistake – no matter where in the progression they are played.

* There are two kinds of harmonizing notes: WAILING NOTES and NOTES OF RESOLUTION. Notes of Resolution establish home base and resolve tension. Wailing Notes move the music away from home base and create tension.

* To play bluesy patterns of notes (also known as riffs, runs, and licks), emphasize Wailing Notes and Notes of Resolution. Use non-harmonizing Stepping Stone Notes as links between these Wailers and Resolvers.

* To figure out which key of harmonica to use when playing Cross Harp, find out what key the music is in. If the music you're accompanying is in, say, the key of **A** count up four steps...

A B C D
1 2 3 4

...and play a **D** harp.

FOUR

Cave Jam: How to Accompany

Travel back 10,000 years to that musty cave where The Cave Boys are laying down some good tunes. Bring your harmonica and play some simple accompaniment. Hey, you play pretty good!

Cave Jam

It was a large, comfortable cave high in the hills above a broad valley. This was where the Cave Boys practiced. The sounds of their instruments would echo loudly off the cave walls. But because the cave was far away from the homes of other cave men, there were few complaints about noise.

It was Sunday afternoon, and the Cave Boys were getting ready to play. This was a new song, written by Krok, the band's lead guitar player and singer. The song was in the key of **G**. *

Counting up four steps, **G** (1) **A** (2) **B** (3) **C** (4), Stone was prepared to boogie on his **C** harp.

Krok's fingers formed a **G** chord on his guitar. "You guys ready?" he asked.

"Yeah," said the big drummer, Smash.

Gref, the bass player, nodded. Stone softly tapped his **C** harp in the palm of his hand.

"Okay," said Krok, "One-two-three-four!"

Whang bam thump thump!! The I-IV-V chord progression started with 4 beats in the chord of **G**. This was the I Chord of Resolution.

As the fourth beat came down, Krok swung his guitar low across his body and changed his **G** chord to a chord in the key of **C**. This was the IV Stepping Stone Chord and the music stayed here for 4 beats. *Whamma bam bam!* slammed the drums as the music returned to the **G**, this time for 8 beats.

"Yeah!" shouted Smash, big arms flailing as he pounded his cymbals and snare drums.

Krok's long fingers danced to the **C** chord for 8 beats and returned to the **G** chord for 8 more.

Here in the **G**, the chord progression seemed to be asking for a change, and a change is what it got. The Cave Boy guitarist nodded to his bass player, jumped lightly from the dirt cave floor, and played a **D** chord, the Dominant Wailer V Chord of the I-IV-V chord progression. This **D** chord gave the music a feeling of movement, of going somewhere. The **D** lasted 4 beats. Then the chord cycle swung down to the **C** chord for 4 tense beats. Oh yeah!

Krok slammed out the **G** chord as the blues cycle came home to the I Chord of Resolution. Four beats passed and the cycle was almost complete. But what's this? With only 4 beats left in the blues cycle, Krok returned to his Dominant Wailer, the **D** chord.

67

"Turn it around!" shouted Smash. The tension wailed for one-two-three-four beats – and at exactly the right moment, the music dove home to the **G** chord for a dramatic resolution of the old cycle and the start of a new one.

This was the TWELVE BAR BLUES CYCLE, a special I-IV-V chord progression that even today is almost always heard when a band plays the slow blues. But Krok didn't care about that. He wanted to hear his harp player. "C'mon Stonie boy," he shouted.   "C'mon!"

Stone began by playing Wailing Note 4 draw. As the I-IV-V chord progression moved through its cycle, each chord change gave the 4 draw new meaning and feeling – almost as though he were changing notes. Because this wailing 4 draw was a harmonizing note, it never made a mistake.

Then, as the cycle neared resolution (and Stone's lungs were about to explode), the fiesty harp player went to the Note of Resolution, 3 blow. The 3 blow and the I Chord of Resolution hit at exactly the same time. Wow!

Now, as the cycle started around again, Stone tongued his 3 blow Note of Resolution, *beating* a rhythm, *phrasing* his sounds the way a singer phrases words. Stone tongued this 3 blow through the entire cycle.

As the cycle started up once more, Stone began playing other Cross Harp harmonizing notes. He played the 6 draw Wailer. He took a run up to the 9 blow Note of Resolution and played his harp down, curling over the notes to Note of Resolution 3 blow. Because he accented the Notes of Resolution and Wailing Notes and played the Stepping Stone Notes lightly, like rungs on a ladder between the harmonizers, he never made a mistake.

"Alright!" shouted Krok as the cycle came to a close. The guitarist opened his mouth wide and started to sing. He might not have had the best voice in the world, but when it came to grunting, groaning, moaning and screaming, no one did it better.

G *(guitar chords)*   **C**
"I've got the Cave Boy Blues, and wouldn't it be fine?"

G
(Stone tongued his 3 blow for 8 beats)

C
"I've got the Cave Boy blues, and wouldn't it be fine?"

G
(Stone played 3 blow, moved to 4 draw and wailed for 8 beats)

D   **C**   **G**
"If you'd pay a little visit to Krokie boy's cave sometime."

G   **D**   **G**
(Stone tongued 3 blow, wailed on 4 draw, slid up to 6 draw, resolved on 6 blow)

"Alright!" shouted Krok, sounding a little like a man with his leg caught in a meat grinder.

Now Stone played a solo of low notes. He drew and tongued hole number one. He blew on hole two and sucked a clear single note on Note of Resolution 2 draw.

His 2 draw slipped up to 3 draw. By changing the shape of his mouth and throat, Stone sucked that note deep into his gut. The 3 draw dipped down to a "bent" 3 draw.* This was the 2½ blues harmonizing note discovered by Adam. It sounded soooo good.

The blues cycle was coming around to the Dominant Wailer. Stone jumped up to holes 4 and 5 draw. These were the tension creating Wailing Notes, the single note expressions of the V Dominant Wailer Chord. Stone swivelled his harmonica back and forth between 4 and 5 draw without stopping his breath.

He continued this 4 and 5 single note draw slide through the IV chord, slipping the harp back and forth like a typewriter carriage between moist Cave Boy lips. It was a small subtle move, but what a sound it made!

Then, as the cycle came home, Stone came home to the 6 blow Note of Resolution. He played 6 draw as the cycle turned around with the Dominant Wailer V Chord, and blew home with a wild flurry of notes that somehow landed on the 3 blow at exactly the same moment that Krok dropped to his knees, clutched his guitar to his chest, and started to sing:

G   **C**
"I've got the Cave Boy blues, and wouldn't it be great?"

G
(Stone drew a long 3 draw bent down for 7 beats and played 3 blow on the 8th beat)

C
"I've got the Cave Boy blues and wouldn't it be great?"

---

* More about bending in Chapter VII

G
(Stone played 1 draw, 2 blow, 2 draw and made that 2 draw talk
until the 8th beat)

D   **C**   **G**
"If you'd consent to be this cave boy's date."

G   **D**   **G**
(Stone played 4 draw, 4 blow, 3 draw, 4 blow, 3 draw, 2 draw)

Stone caressed home his 2 draw Note of Resolution and took off
on a new solo. Smash double thumped his drums and Gref's low
bass notes drove home a deep blues feeling. Round and round went
the I-IV-V chord progression, this twelve bar blues cycle.
Stone's harmonica growled like a wildcat, howled like a coyote,
moaned like a lover who wanted more. It was incredible.

Stone even played the Six Blow Down, a harp riff using Adam's
Blues Scale – only in reverse. Note of Resolution 6 blow was the 1st
note. Five draw was the 6½ note. Four draw served as the wailing
5th note. Four blow was the 4th note. Three draw bent down was
the 2½ blues harmonizing note, and 3 blow, another Note of
Resolution, was the 1st note of the scale.

Blues Scale Down
6 ⑤④ 4 ③ 3

71

As the music swelled and reverberated off the musty walls, the other band members just looked at each other. Stone's music sounded so good it was hard to concentrate.

How could he do all that on a tiny harmonica?

Finally, Krok could stand it no longer. He put his guitar down, unplugged it from his electric tree stump. "Tell me..." he gasped, "Tell me...how did you do that?"

Stone smiled. "What key is the next song in?" Then he turned away and acted busy. A harp player never reveals his or her secrets – unless there's cash involved.

Finally, Stone agreed to teach the Cave Boys how to play Cross Harp for 20 clams a person. Fresh, *plump* clams. And he'd even let them use his harps.

Notes

* Music moves in circles. The circle almost always plays the same chord pattern again and again. This is a CHORD PROGRESSION. Most chord progressions are built around the I-IV-V pattern.

* To jam with a band, guitarist, or a record, find out where the music begins and ends. This is the KEY you're playing in.

* Select the CORRECT KEY HARMONICA. To play Cross Harp, count up 4 steps from the key the music is in. If the music is in the key of **G**, play a **C** harp. If the music is in the key of **E**, play an **A** harp.

* Get a FEEL for the music before you start your accompaniment. Let the rhythm flow through your body. Get a sense of the chord progression's circular motion.

* A good way to START YOUR ACCOMPANIMENT is to play a long 4 draw. Hear how each chord change gives new meaning and feeling to this harmonizing note.

* GO SLOW AND HAVE A GOOD TIME.

FIVE

Stone's Harmonica Lesson: Blues and Rock Riffs

Riffs are patterns of notes that always sound bluesy and musical. They connect Notes of Resolution, Wailing Notes and Stepping Stone Notes to help you make music as you blow and draw your way around the harmonica. Some of the riffs in Chapter V are too difficult to play immediately. Don't let this stop you from tooting along and having a good time.

The Lesson Begins

Stone told the Cave Boys how Wailing Notes create musical tension and Notes of Resolution resolve tension. He told them how Stepping Stone Notes were used as links, or rungs on a ladder, between Wailing Notes and Notes of Resolution. Still, the band was impatient.

"Okay," growled Smash, "Now we know which notes create tension and which notes resolve it. What are we supposed to do? Play them all at the same time?"

"Take it easy," said Stone. "Let's take Wailing Note 4 draw and Note of Resolution 3 blow. We know you can play either one – and they'll always work when you accompany a I-IV-V chord progression." He picked up his harmonica and played the Beginner's Blues Riff.

"If playing 3 blow and 4 draw always works, why not build a ladder, using 3 draw and 4 blow as Stepping Stones? Like this:"

76

He handed each of the Cave Boys a small diatonic harmonica. "Now you guys try it...but don't spit too much in the harps. It clogs them up."

Each of the Cave Boys tried to play the Up Riff.

But instead of the smooth, rich tone Stone got from his harmonica, all the Cave Boys could produce was a cacophony of hisses, bleats, and honks.

It sounded like an invasion of geese.

"C'mon you guys," said Stone. "You gotta get a good single note before you can play a lick. You gotta pucker, like this..."

Stone pushed his lips out so they formed a verticle oval.

"...and see, you put the harmonica well inside your mouth. Push it up a little bit – towards your nose – so your upper lip doesn't have to stretch so much."

He looked at Smash, whose face was set in a determined grimace. "Smash!" he shouted.

But it was too late. Smash removed the harmonica from his mouth. It was crushed to smithereens – bent by the pressure of the big drummer's clenched lips.

"You gotta relax!" shouted Stone. "You gotta mellow out with those big lips of yours!"

He looked sadly at the crushed harmonica.

"Okay," he finally sighed. "Let's try again. Blow and draw on hole 3; blow and draw on hole 4. Remember, 4 draw is your Wailing Note, so play the 3 blow, 3 draw and 4 blow quickly and smoothly. Then, when you get to the 4 draw, stretch it out. Waaaaaiiiillllllllllll."

Once again the Cave Boys played the Up Riff. This time it sounded a lot better, though there were still many missed notes and strange honking sounds.

"That's a little better," said Stone. "But I don't see what's so hard about it. You blow and draw on 3. You blow and draw on 4, and you hold the 4 draw a long time to create tension."

The Cave Boys went at it again. Sure enough, they could hear the blues in this simple pattern of notes. In fact, a few of the times they tried it, even Stone was impressed. Of course, he didn't tell them.

Those crazy dudes might think they already know how to play harp. They might decide to forget about the lesson. And Stone could taste those clams.

The Down Riff

"Now that you're playing a riff that takes you up your harmonica, I'm gonna show you one that takes you down," said Stone. "All you've got to do is play the Up Riff in reverse. And dig it, you've got a hot blues lick."

"That's it," Stone said as the Cave Boys played their own versions of the Down Riff.

"Now, 4 draw is a Wailing Note, so play it a long time. Maybe two beats, eh? The 4 blow is a Stepping Stone Note so play it quickly and move to the 3 draw. The 3 draw is a Wailer. You can really create tension with this little bugger, so hold it out. Try to create a sense of anticipation for the 3 blow. Then, after 2 or 3 beats (depending on how it feels best to you), play 3 blow."

"And the Down Riff is like the Up Riff? It will always sound good when accompanying a I-IV-V chord progression?" asked Krok.

"Of course," said Stone, "As long as it accents the Wailing Notes and Notes of Resolution."

"Prove it," said Krok. He picked up his guitar and began playing. His fingers leapt from chord to chord. First he played a **G** chord, then an **A** minor chord, then a **C** chord and lastly a **D**.

"Hey!" said Smash, "That's not a I-IV-V chord progression."

"It's close enough," said Stone. "As long as the music stays in the same key, these harmonica riffs will work. All you have to do is *mold* them to the music.

As Krok strummed the chords, Stone played the Down Riff as fast as he could, over and over. It fit perfectly with the music.

Then he played it very slowly, putting a big accent on the 3 draw Wailing Note. Again, it sounded great with guitar music.

Next, Stone played the Down Riff so the 4 draw lasted 12 beats, the 4 blow and 3 draw occurred in 1 beat and the resolving 3 blow was played for 3 beats.

Now Krok changed his chord progression. He stayed in the key of **G**, but his fingers jumped to the **F** chord, back to the **G**, to the **F**, back to the **G**. Then he went to the **E** minor chord, the **A** minor chord, to the **D** chord, and finally back to the **G** chord.

"Whew!" said Smash. But Stone kept right on playing the Down Riff. As he played the Cave Boys gradually realized that what Stone said was true. Any riff that puts the accent on a Wailing Note or Note of Resolution will sound terrific when accompanying a blues or rock n' roll chord progression.

"You see, boys," the harp player finally said, "These riffs aren't exact. They're basic moves you can make on your harp. But *how* you make the move depends on the music you're accompanying, and what feels best to you."

"But how do you know what riff to play next?" asked Smash.

"Dig it," Stone replied. "Playing harp is like being in a good conversation. You don't know what you're going to say next; and if you tried to plan it, you'd probably get tongue-tied.

"You'll learn the language. Then you let what comes out of your mouth be a complete surprise. You catch on to the flow and feeling of the music and trust yourself.

"And if you make a mistake, say, playing 5 draw instead of 4 draw, don't worry about it. Just incorporate the 5 draw into the music.

Invent your own blues lick."

"How?" asked Krok.

"Lots of ways. But the most obvious is by sliding back to the 4 draw and wailing. The result would be:

Five Draw Mistake

Stone played the 5 Draw Mistake.

"Hey, that's pretty good," said Smash. "I guess mistakes aren't really so bad after all."

"Not when you make them on purpose," winked Stone.

More Music on Holes
Three and Four

"In case you haven't noticed," said Stone, "Holes 3 and 4 are a veritable orchestra. There are so many patterns to play here that I couldn't begin to count them all.

"For instance, you can join the Up Riff and the Down Riff so they form one lick: the Up and Down Blues Riff."

"The Up and Down Blues Riff starts out on Note of Resolution 3 blow. The 3 blow lets you know where home base is, where the music starts and ends. Then you take the Up Riff to the 4 draw Wailing Note. Play this 4 draw a long time to create tension.

"Then (and this is important), you pause. End of the Up Riff. Enter the Down Riff. Four draw, 4 blow, now a long moan of a 3 draw that creates tension...and FINALLY your Note of Resolution 3 blow.

"Now you guys try it."

It was hard work teaching these Neanderthals to play Cross Harp. But one thing about cave men, they were willing to work hard. Thus, in a couple of hours, all the Cave Boys (even Smash, who paid an extra 5 clams for a new harp) were sounding pretty good on the Up and Down Riff.

Stone threw another piece of wood on the fire. Smoke billowed through the cave. "Okay," he coughed, "Now I'm going to show you guys some new licks and patterns on holes 3 and 4."

He squatted on the dirt floor of the cave and used a twig to draw some primitive diagrams.

"For instance, instead of playing 4 draw, 4 blow, 3 draw, 3 blow, play 4 draw, 4 blow, 3 draw, 4 *draw*. That's right. Instead of resolving tension, slide back to the 4 draw Wailer – and create tension."

Four Draw Surprise
④ 4 ③④

"You can play the 4 Draw Surprise over and over, and it will always fit in with the I-IV-V chord progression. Then, when you're tired of creating tension, finish your pattern with a 3 blow.

"And it sounds real good to alternate the 4 Draw Surprise with the Up Riff and the Down Riff. Like this..."

Stone put his harp to his mouth, puckered, and began to play in a clear, throbbing tone.

④ 4 ③ 3 (Down Riff)
④ 4 ③④ (4 Draw Surprise)
3 ③ 4 ④ (Up Riff)
④ 3 ③ 3 (Down Riff)

"Hey!" shouted Krok, "That sounds just like a little blues song!"

"Of course," said Stone. "That is because the first riff established home base, the next two riffs created tension, and the final riff returned to home base."

"And you did all that on two harmonica holes," said Smash. Thinking of the ton load of drums he had to carry around just to make a little music, he shook his head slowly.

"Maybe I've been playing the wrong instrument," he said.

"Careful," laughed Stone. "There's only one harp player in this band."

Two Draw

"Here's one of the best licks I know," said Stone. "I call it the Good Morning Riff because it sounds snappy and bright. It uses 2 draw as a Note of Resolution. Two draw is the same note as 3 blow. I find I use 2 draw when I'm playing a riff that comes from the bottom of the harp (such as the Good Morning Riff), and that I use the 3 blow Note of Resolution when I play a riff in the midrange of the harp (such as the Down Riff)."

Stone played the Good Morning Riff a few times. Sure enough, it did sound snappy and bright. But when the Cave Boys tried, the riff sounded like it hadn't had a good night's sleep in weeks. The trouble was with the 2 draw. None of the beginning harp players could get a sound out of the rebellious note.

"What the heck's wrong with my 2 draw?" Smash asked. He peered angrily into the little square hole.

"The low draw notes give everyone trouble," Stone said. "The tendency is to tighten up when you suck on them. When they don't respond, the tendency is to suck even harder. Good way to break your harp.

"But if you want to play 2 draw right, try this. Take your harp out of your mouth. Now, rub your lips. Pinch them. Pucker up. Now relax...

"Consider, gentlemen, if you placed a straw up to that 2 draw and gently sucked, the note would play perfectly. But the way *you* go about playing the 2 draw Note of Resolution, forcing the air into your throat, you can't even get a sound. Hah!

"Put your harp back into your mouth, push it up towards your nose. Gently, very gently, draw a controlled stream of air to the roof of your mouth. *Coax* that note out. Keep the feeling light and airy. That note will come, but you gotta persuade it."

Armed with this new advice, the Cave Boys went to work on the 2 draw. Gref got it first – probably because he was a more relaxed type of guy. But before long, all the Cave Boys were playing the 2 draw, and the Good Morning Riff.

"Like any riff I show you," said Stone, "The Good Morning Riff can be played with many variations. Try tonguing the 2 draw in triplets: ① 2 ②(triplet).

"Or bounce back and forth between the 2 draw and the 2 blow: ① 2 ② 2 ②

"You also can use the Good Morning Riff as a starting place for a pattern that takes you up to 3 draw."

Good Morning Three Draw
① 2 ② ③

"Or, you can continue the riff up to 4 draw."

Good Morning Four Draw
① 2 ② ③ 4 ④

"But for simple accompaniment to a song you don't know that well, the Good Morning Riff ending on 2 draw: 1 draw, 2 blow, 2 draw — with a little tonguing action thrown in on the 2 draw is the safest way to go. Play it over and over, changing the timing and feeling to fit the music. It will never make a mistake."

Surprise Resolution

"If you've been paying attention," Stone said, "You've probably noticed that most of the Cross Harp riffs I've shown you are built around a Note of Resolution.

"The Up Riff, the Down Riff, the Four Draw Surprise – all use the 3 blow. The Good Morning Riff uses the 2 draw.

"Now I want to show you a couple of riffs that resolve on the 6 blow Note of Resolution. Six blow is the same note as 2 draw or 3 blow, but it's up an octave. (See page 16) You can toot along on 6 blow through an entire song and never make a mistake.

"The first riff we should try is the Surprise Resolution. It starts as though you were playing the Down Riff: 4 draw, 4 blow, 3 draw... but instead of resolving on 3 blow, slide the harp up to Note of Resolution 6 blow. Like this:

"Not bad," said Krok after he'd played the Surprise Resolution a few times. "It doesn't do what you'd expect, but it sounds good anyway. What else can you do with the 6 blow?"

"Why not go into the 6 draw?" suggested Gref. "I see here on your Cross Harp Map that it's a Wailing Note. Maybe I can create tension on the 6 draw and resolve it on the 6 blow."

Gref played a long cry on the 6 draw. Then, very gently, he brought it home to the Note of Resolution, 6 blow.

Six Draw and Blow Resolution
⑥ 6

"That's really sweet," said Krok. "But here's an idea. Tongue the 6 draw to create even more tension."

The shaggy-haired guitarist put the harp in his mouth, puckered to get a clear single note, and drew on hole 6. Keeping one long draw, he tongued *ta ta taaaaaaa*.

Then, he stopped and looked at the rest of the Cave Boys with a sly smile.

"C'mon..." complained Smash.

"If you don't play that 6 blow, I will," said Gref.

Stone threw his head back and laughed. "Boy, that 6 draw sure created tension. I mean, it's still hanging there in the air. Somebody's got to resolve it."

"I can't stand it," Smash said. He played the 6 blow. There was a tremendous sense of release, of resolution, a feeling of being able to breathe again.

Krok looked at his harmonica in amazement. "Hey, this is a powerful little thing, isn't it?"

Good Old Six Blow

"Here's a nice little lick that will take you from Note of Resolution 6 Blow Down to Note of Resolution 3 blow," said Stone. "It's kinda like a scale:"

Tapping his foot 1 – 2 – 1 – 2 Stone played the 6 Blow Down a few times. "Now, one of the tricks in playing this lick is the way you move the harp from 5 draw to 4 draw. You SLIDE the harp, continuing to draw. If you do it by drawing on hole 5, stopping the draw, moving the harp to hole 4, and starting your draw again, the riff will sound clumsy."

"See what you mean," said Gref after he slowly played the 6 Blow Down. "What do you call that?"

"A DRAW SLIDE," said Stone. "It's one of those little details that can make a huge difference. And heck, it's not hard to keep drawing as you move the harp. Sure improves your music, though."

---

* Six Blow Down is Adam's Blues Scale played in reverse.

The Cave Boys played with the 6 Blow Down for several minutes, stomping out a $1-2-1-2$ rhythm and putting the riff into this rhythmic framework.

After everyone had the hang of it, Stone said, "Now another thing you can do is stop the riff on 4 draw and create tension."

"And then you can resolve your tension using either the Good Morning Riff (1 draw, 2 blow, 3 blow), the Down Riff (4 draw, 4 blow, 3 draw, 3 blow), the Surprise Resolution (4 draw, 4 blow, 3 draw, 6 blow), or any other way of getting to a Note of Resolution you might discover."

"So tell me," said Gref, "When you play, do you think to yourself, 'Now I'm gonna play the Surprise Resolution, now I'm gonna create tension on 6 draw?' "

"I never do that," said Stone. "It would petrify me to play harp and think at the same time. No, playing harp is like dancing. You just blow and draw, warble and wail, and it comes out the way it's supposed to. And even if it isn't perfect, you still have a good time.

"And isn't that the whole point of playing music – to have a good time?"

"Then what's the purpose of learning all these riffs?" asked Smash. "Why not just pick the ol' harmonica up and play it?"

"I think you should," replied Stone. "When you practice, you should get your $1-2-1-2$ beat going, try a few of the licks you've learned from me, then leave those behind and play your own. After a few minutes of *not using* the stuff you've memorized, try the riffs again, always keeping your two stomp beat.

"By going back and forth between memorizing and being spontaneous, you'll be teaching yourself and having a good time. After a few days of working this way, the licks you've memorized will have become part of the way you pick the harp up and play it. They'll be natural. Know what I mean?"

Stone looked at his watch, a small Timex strapped to his wrist with dinosaur sinew. "Listen fellows, it's been hours. Haven't I earned my clams yet?"

"Is there more to the harmonica?" asked Krok.

"Well...of course," said Stone. "But it would take hours to cover everything: bending notes, how to use your hands, how to play these riffs in a I-IV-V blues cycle, using microphones, amplifiers, playing with records. Don't you think you've heard enough?"

"What about the notes above 6 draw?" Krok persisted.

"Well, they're a little more difficult than the notes on holes 1 through 6; but if you want to know about them, I'll tell you."

"If you want your clams," said Smash, "you'll tell us."

Nine Blow

Stone squatted in the dirt of the cave. The fire reflected dual images on his aviator glasses.

"Okay," he began. "Holes 1 through 6 are the nuts and bolts of simple Cross Harp. Still, the holes above 6 will add drama to your harp playing.

"When learning these high notes, it's a good idea to practice on your lower harps: **G**, **A** flat or **A**. Since these harps are pitched a little lower, the high notes aren't nearly as difficult to play."

Stone took an **A** harp from his harmonica bag and played a 9 blow.

Nine Blow

"Nine blow," he said, "is your Note of Resolution. It's the same note as 6 blow, only up an octave. It's the same note as 2 draw and 3 blow, but up two octaves." Stone gave **A** harps to Smash, Gref and Krok and let them work on the high, difficult 9 blow.

"Nine blow feels different than your lower notes," Stone said. "I change the shape of my lips and throat for this one. The airstream feels finely focused, and comes from my head rather than my throat or body as it does for the lower notes."

Nine blows (and pieces of 10 blows and 8 blows) screeched through the cave's musty air. "Takes a while to get the hang of this end of your harp," said Stone. "But it's worth it. There are some good licks up here."

"Such as?" asked Krok.

"Such as the 9 Blow Down," said Stone. "It takes you from the 9 blow Note of Resolution down to the 6 blow Note of Resolution.*

Stone cupped his hands around his harp and played a high, smooth lick starting on the 9 blow, lightly touching the 9 draw, the 8 blow, the 8 draw (creating a tiny bit of tension on this Wailing Note), sliding to the 7 draw, creating tension on the Wailing Note 6 draw and finally resolving on the 6 blow Note of Resolution.

"Remember," said Stone, "On holes 7 through 10, blow notes are higher than draw notes. Practicing the 9 Blow Down will help you get a feeling for this.

---

* Nine Blow Down is the same riff as 6 Blow Down, but is up an octave.

Nine Blow Down
9 ⑨ 8 ⑧ ⑦ ⑥ 6

"Now, let me show you the 6 Blow Up. This is a Cross Harp lick that takes you from 6 blow to 9 blow.

Six Blow Up
6 ⑦⑧ 8 9

Each of the Cave Boy's attempted to play the 6 Blow Up, but the riff was difficult and frustrating – especially getting a clean sound on the 9 blow.

"How long did it take you to learn to play these high notes?" asked Gref.

"Man, I'm still learning," answered Stone. "Lots of times that 9 blow will just take off on me, or I'll try to play it and only get half the note. Sounds awful..."

"I've heard," said Krok.

Through his aviator glasses, Stone gave the lead guitarist a long, hard and dirty look. Even if he was a funky, harp-playing Cave Boy, Stone was a pretty sensitive guy. And, like most musicians, it was a lot easier for him to criticize himself than to hear it from others.

"Oh, yeah?" he finally said. He put his **A** harp to his lips. A long cry of a 9 blow rang out. Then the harp slid down over the notes, bending, twisting, shrieking, descending over the 9 draw, the 8 blow, the 8 draw, the 7 draw, the 6 draw, to the 6 blow, then performing a draw slide through the 5 draw, 4 draw, 3 draw, 2 draw, 1 draw- and back up through the 2 blow, 2 draw, 3 draw, and finally resolving on 2 draw.

"That, my friends, is the Complete Blues Scale Down."

Complete Blues Scale Down

9 ⑨ 8 ⑧⑦⑥ 6 ⑤④③②① 2 ②③②

"And here," he said, "is the popular, amazing, and difficult-to-play Complete Blues Scale Up."

Complete Blues Scale Up
①2②③4④5 6⑦⑧8 9

As Stone started on his 1 draw and moved swiftly and smoothly up the notes to 9 blow, Krok, Gref and Smash eyed each other. What was this guy trying to prove?

"Okay, Krok ol' boy," said Stone when the last echoes of the shrieking 9 blow had died. "It's your turn. Let's hear you play that lick."

"C'mon, man," said Krok. "I'm just starting out on harp. You know I can't play a lick like that."

"Don't have what it takes, eh?"

"Man, I play guitar..."

Stone laughed, "Not as difficult an instrument as harp, I guess."

"Listen, Stone..."

But Stone would not listen to Krok's excuses. Here he had spent hours showing these guys the secrets of Cross Harp, and Krok insults his playing.

"I'll bet you 20 clams you can't play this lick," Stone said.

Before Krok even had time to reply, Stone said, "I'll bet you *60* clams you can't play this lick."

Krok looked at the little harmonica resting in his hand. Its wooden edges and engraved hole numbers glistened in the firelight. He asked himself, could he play the Complete Blues Scale Up? Just once? Could he get lucky? Hmmmmmm 60 clams.

"Okay," he finally said. "You got a bet."

The Bet

Krok stood in the center of the cave. His face was streaked with sweat. His legs felt weak.

"Look," Gref said, "If you want to chicken out I'm sure Stone will..."

Krok hardly heard his worried bass player. He was deep inside himself, gathering his powers of concentration. Then, hands trembling, he cupped the boo boo reed beauty and put it to his puckered lips. Very softly, he played the 1 draw. A timid tone came from the harp. One draw. So far so good.

Knowing 1 draw was a Wailing Note, that he could play it as long as he wanted, Krok gently drew air through the reed inside the harp. (Since you know this same vital secret of Cross Harp, you might want to play your 1 draw as you read. It would give the story a nice musical backdrop.)

Now, from 1 draw, Krok would have to hop lightly to Stepping Stone 2 blow before he could find another safe spot. This would be Note of Resolution 2 draw.

①² ②

He mentally rehearsed this small move of his harmonica and the draw-blow-draw transition required to get to the Note of Resolution. Okay, he finally said to himself, let's do it.

He moved the harmonica to hole 2. He blew and then he sucked. Two draw rang through. He made it. He was safe. For now.

As he drew on Note of Resolution 2 draw, he planned his next move. From the 2 draw, he'd have to go to 3 draw, continue on to hole 4, blow, and immediately draw – ending up, theoretically, on Wailing Note 4 draw. Another safe spot that would always work.

②③⁴ ④

Okay. He was going for it. Carefully, he slid the harp from the 2 draw to the 3 draw. Being a Wailing Note (usually used as a Stepping Stone in this lick), the 3 draw gave him time to think.

Yeah, the voice in his head told him, move the harp to hole 4 at the same time that you blow. Then draw. Yeah, Krok, you can do it. With a gentle pull he moved the harp to hole 4 as he blew and sucked. Perfect! He was playing the 4 draw. No one thought he'd make it to 2 draw and here he was, wailing on the 4 draw. He opened his eyes and looked across the firelit cave where Stone watched through flame-licked aviator glasses. What Krok would give to read his mind now.

Ta ta ta. He flicked his tongue on the fleshy ridge behind his teeth as he drew the 4 draw reed. *Ta ta ta*.

Might as well create a little tension while I'm here, he said to himself. *Ta ta ta*.

Ah, but this was no time for messing around. He had to think. (And if thinking is tough for 20th Century man, consider what it must have been like for a Cave Boy.)

Now, this next move would not be as difficult. All he would have to do is move the harp to hole 5 and blow. Still blowing, he'd continue moving the harp to hole 6. And there he'd be – playing the 6 blow Note of Resolution.

④ 5 6

This is it, he thought. Gently he moved the harp to hole 5 and blew. Without breaking stride, he slid the harmonica to hole 6.

And there he was on 6 blow. *Ta ta ta*. His tongue tapped triumphantly on the moist ridge of his mouth just above his upper teeth. *Ta ta tatty ta taaaaah!*

What now?

Okay, he thought. First off, remember that the order of notes above 6 draw is reversed. From now on, blows are going to be higher than draws.

As for the move itself, it really didn't look that difficult. From the 6 blow Note of Resolution, slide the harp to hole 7 and draw. Continue sliding the harp to 8 draw.

6 ⑦ ⑧

Eight draw wasn't the most effective Wailing Note on the harp, but it would do for now. It would *have* to.

Bonzai, Cave Boy...

From the 6 blow, he sucked and moved the harp to hole 7 and to hole 8. Made it. But there was no time for congratulations. Eight draw just didn't sound that good as a Wailing Note.

But he was almost home. Almost 60 clams richer. All he'd have to do now was blow on hole 8 and blow on 9. Yeah. Go for it!

So he did. He blew on the 8 and slid the harp to the 9. There he was – playing the 9 blow Note of Resolution. He had done it. He had actually played the Complete Blues Scale Up!

Still playing the 9 blow (wanting to savor the moment), Krok looked across the cave at Stone. To his surprise, the wirey harp player was smiling broadly. Hmmmmm, thought Krok, maybe Stone isn't such a bad guy after all.

"Yeah, man!" shouted Smash. He looked down at the tiny harmonica almost lost in his huge hand. If Krok could do it, so could he. The trick was to go real slow and to rest on the Wailing Note and Notes of Resolution.

"Right on," said Gref. He, too, was looking excitedly at his harmonica.

Ta ta ta! cried Krok's 9 blow. He made the note crow like a rooster, bark like a dog, wail like a fire engine. *Ta ta tatty ta taaaaah!* The triumphant 9 blow bounced and echoed off the cave walls. To all the Cave Boys, even Stone, the sound of this Note of Resolution was a thing of great beauty, a symbol of man's conquest over the unknown, a tribute to his ability to learn new skills.

Krok lowered the harp from his lips and smiled. Then he collapsed to the cave floor. Poor guy hadn't taken a decent breath in what seemed like hours.

~~~

If you've been playing along while reading, be certain you breathe once in a while. And if you *have* been having trouble with your breathing, The Sensuous Harp Player (Chapter VII) should be of great value to you.

Notes

* There is no one way to play any of these riffs. The idea is to MOLD them to the music, to the beat, to your mood.

* When you make a mistake, DON'T STOP PLAYING. Simply continue blowing and drawing until you get to a Note of Resolution or a Wailing Note. When in doubt, fake it.

* When practicing these blues riffs, keep a steady $1-2-1-2$ or $1-2-3-4$ beat going with your foot.

* Use TONGUING to add rhythm and tension to Wailing Notes and Notes of Resolution.

* SIMPLICITY and REPETITION are important features of good harp music. For instance, the Good Morning Riff played again and again will usually sound better than the Complete Blues Scale Down or Complete Blues Scale Up.

* Feel free to use the patterns in this chapter as inspiration for making up your own blues patterns.

* Some of the riffs in this chapter are quite difficult. Don't feel you need to be able to play them before reading on.

* A tape cassette lesson teaching you these riffs is available from the Cross Harp Press.

SIX

Three Chords of the Blues: Playing Solo

Say good bye to that ancient cave where you learned your first blues riffs and pucker up to modern day harmonica music. Chapter VI gets you playing solo harp in I-IV-V blues cycles. Quite possibly this is the most important chapter in the book. Enjoy.

Solo Harp

There you are, playing your harmonica all by yourself, playing *solo*. You play the Up Riff. You play the Down Riff. You play the Blues Scale Down. You play the Good Morning Riff. The riffs you've been practicing sound great, but how do you link them together into one cohesive jam?

When you're playing with a guitar or a piano, there doesn't seem to be any problem. That's because these instruments play the chords and chord cycles. All the harp does is accompany.

But when you're playing by yourself, it's more difficult. The question you ask yourself is: which riff do I play now?

There are many approaches to playing solo harp music. You can play riffs to create and resolve tension. An example of this is playing the Up Riff (ending on Wailing Note 4 draw), pausing, and playing the Down Riff (resolving the tension on 3 blow).

You can play to create a rhythmic effect. You can do this by tonguing one note, say 3 blow, to a staccato train rhythm, using the Up Riff to wail on 4 draw, and returning to the rhythmic 3 blow.

You can also play your blues riffs in cycles – specifically I-IV-V cycles. When you play your solo music in a I-IV-V cycle, the I Chord of Resolution establishes home base. The IV Stepping Stone Chord moves the music away from home. The Dominant Wailer V Chord moves the music further still. Returning to the I Chord of Resolution provides a sense of completion of the cycle and can also signify the start of a new cycle.

Here's a simple I-IV-V chord cycle for Cross Harp. It's so short and easy you could call it a mini-cycle. Stomping out a 1 – 2 – 1 – 2 beat, play this cycle over and over. Give each chord two beats. Add tonguing to give special feeling. Imagine these sounds as a musical wheel and make that wheel roll.

Single Note Cycles

Playing Cross Harp, the single notes that express the I Chord of Resolution are the Notes of Resolution 2 draw, 3 blow, 6 blow and 9 blow.

The notes that express the IV Stepping Stone Chord are Stepping Stone Notes 1 blow, 4 blow, 7 blow and 10 blow.

The single notes expressing the V Dominant Wailer Chord are Wailing Notes 1 draw, 4 draw and 8 draw. Three draw bent down and 6 draw will also work.

Giving each note two beats, play this I-IV-V single note mini-cycle.

3	4	④	3
Resolution	Stepping	Wailing	Resolution
I	IV	V	I

Here's a mini-cycle that has you play the Wailing Note before you play the Stepping Stone Note.

3	④	4	3
Resolution	Wailing	Stepping	Resolution
I	V	IV	I

Try tonguing every note in this mini-cycle twice. Try tonguing in triplets. Tongue as though the harp were having a conversation with itself, making some sounds long and others short. No matter what your tonguing pattern, give each note two steady stomps of your foot. Make that harp go!

Single note progressions can also be played on the low end of your harp. Two draw is the same note as 3 blow. One blow is the same note as 4 blow, but an octave lower. Also one octave down, 1 draw is the same note as 4 draw.

② 1 ① ②
Resolution Stepping Wailing Resolution
I IV V I

Tonguing every note of the above progression will get your rhythm going. NOT tonguing the final 2 draw will produce a stronger feeling of resolution. Keep that foot, mouth and breath going as you play progression over and over.

Twelve Bars That Sound So Good

Anyone who listens to the blues has heard the 12 bar blues cycle. It's a long, slow progression with a steady 4 stomp beat. The term "12 bars" refers to 12 sections, each consisting of 4 beats. Playing clear single notes and stomping 1 – 2 – 3 – 4 – 1 – 2 – 3 – 4, play this single note blues cycle again and again. Tonguing each note will help make it more bluesy.

Twelve Bars for Beginner's Cycle

I	Note of Resolution	3	(4 Beats)
IV	Stepping Stone Note	4	(4 Beats)
I	Note of Resolution	3	(4 Beats)
I	Note of Resolution	3	(4 Beats)
IV	Stepping Stone Note	4	(4 Beats)
IV	Stepping Stone Note	4	(4 Beats)
I	Note of Resolution	3	(4 Beats)
I	Note of Resolution	3	(4 Beats)
V	Dominant Wailer Note	④	(4 Beats)
IV	Stepping Stone Note	4	(4 Beats)
I	Note of Resolution	3	(4 Beats)
V	Dominant Wailer	④	(4 Beats)

(Start the cycle again)

Riff Cycles

The next stage in playing dynamite solo Cross Harp to the I-IV-V progression is to use riffs that:

1. End on a Note of Resolution to express the I chord.
2. End on Stepping Stone Note 1 blow, 4 blow, 7 blow or 10 blow to express the IV chord.
3. End on Wailing Note 1 draw, 4 draw, 6 draw, 8 draw or 3 draw bent down to express the V chord.

For instance, the Down Riff ends on 3 blow. Use it as a Riff of Resolution.

Down Riff
④ 4 ③ 3

To express the IV chord, play a riff that ends on a Stepping Stone Note, say, 4 blow.

④④④ 4

Tongue the 4 draw three times, then play 4 blow.

To play a Dominant Wailer V Riff, use Wailing Note 4 draw in the Up Riff.

Up Riff
3 ③ 4 ④

Resolve your blues cycle with the Down Riff, giving the home base 3 blow a feeling of finality and completion.

Down Riff
④ 4 ③ 3

Try playing these riffs so they create a blues cycle.

Beginner's Blues Cycle

I	Riff of Resolution	④ 4 ③ 3
IV	Stepping Stone Riff	④④④ 4
V	Dominant Wailer Riff	3 ③ 4 ④
I	Riff of Resolution	④ 4 ③ 3

You can play the Wailing V Riff BEFORE you play the Stepping Stone IV Riff and get another simple blues progression.

Stomp N' Tongue Blues Cycle

I	Riff of Resolution	④ 4 ③ 3
V	Dominant Wailer Riff	3 ③ 4 ④
IV	Stepping Stone Riff	④④④ 4
I	Riff of Resolution	④ 4 ③ 3

On the low end of your harp, use 2 draw to end your Riff of Resolution, 1 blow as a Stepping Stone Riff ending, and 4 draw to put the wail in your Wailing Riff.

Good Morning Blues Cycle

I	Riff of Resolution	① 2 ②②
IV	Stepping Stone Riff	2 3 2 1
V	Dominant Wailer Riff	④ 4 ③④
I	Riff of Resolution	④ 4 ③ 3

Another way to play the I-IV-V cycle is to use 6 blow to end your Riff of Resolution and 6 draw to create the Dominant Wailer Riff.

Blues for Pamina Cycle

I	Riff of Resolution	⑥ 6 ⑤④ 4 ③ 3
IV	Stepping Stone Riff	④④④ 4
V	Dominant Wailer Riff	④⑤ 6 ⑥
I	Riff of Resolution	⑥⑥⑥ 6

108

More Solo Cycles

Here are some blues cycles that use more than four riffs. Pause between riffs if you want, but keep the beat going.

Prosperity Blues Cycle

I	Riff of Resolution	3 ③ 4 ④
		④ 4 ③ 3
IV	Stepping Stone Riff	④④④ 4
I	Riff of Resolution	④ 4 ③ 3
V	Dominant Wailer	④④④④
IV	Stepping Stone Riff	④④④ 4
I	Riff of Resolution	④ 4 ③ 3
V	Dominant Wailer	3 ③ 4 ④
	or	
I	Riff of Resolution	3 ③③ 3

This blues cycle can be concluded by playing the Riff of Resolution twice. Or, it can be continued by playing the Riff of Resolution once and then playing a Wailing Riff. Playing this Wailing Riff at the end of the blues cycle is called a TURN-AROUND. The turn-around ends the blues cycle in a state of tension on the V chord, and makes you want to play it again.

The first two times you play the above cycle, use the turn-around. The third time you play it, resolve on the Riff of Resolution.

This next blues cycle uses another combination of Wailing Notes and Notes of Resolution.

Jamaica Blues Cycle

I	Riff of Resolution	⑥⑥⑥ 6
V	Dominant Wailer	6 ⑤④④
IV	Stepping Stone Riff	④⑤④ 4
I	Riff of Resolution	①2②②
V	Dominant Wailer	3 ③4④
IV	Stepping Stone Riff	④④④ 4
I	Riff of Resolution	①2②②

V	Dominant Wailer	②③4④
	or	
I	Riff of Resolution	3 ③③3

This example of a blues cycle uses the high end of your harp. Up here, 9 blow is often used as a Note of Resolution. Eight draw is a Wailing Note, and 7 blow is a Stepping Stone Note.

Tia's Blues Cycle

I	Riff of Resolution	⑧⑨ 9 9
V	Dominant Wailer	9 ⑨ 8⑧
IV	Stepping Stone Riff	⑧⑧⑧ 7
I	Riff of Resolution	⑥⑥⑥ 6
V	Dominant Wailer	6 ⑦ 7⑧
IV	Stepping Stone Riff	⑧9⑨ 7
I	Riff of Resolution	⑥⑥⑥ 6

V	Dominant Wailer	6 ⑦ 7⑧
	or	
I	Riff of Resolution	6 ⑦⑧⑦ 6

Twelve Bar Blues for Harp

Here's a 12 bar blues cycle using simple Cross Harp Riffs. Stomping your foot, try to keep each riff within a 4 beat framework.

Ocean Wave Blues Cycle

I	Riff of Resolution	④ 4 ③ 3
IV	Stepping Stone Riff	④④④ 4
I	Riff of Resolution	④ 4 ③ 3
I	Riff of Resolution	④ 4 ③ 3
IV	Stepping Stone Riff	④④④ 4
IV	Stepping Stone Riff	④④④ 4
I	Riff of Resolution	④ 4 ③ 3
I	Riff of Resolution	④ 4 ③ 3
V	Dominant Wailer Riff	3 ③ 4 ④
IV	Stepping Stone Riff	④④④ 4
I	Riff of Resolution	④ 4 ③ 3
V	Dominant Wailer	3 ③ 4 ④

Play this cycle again and again. Tongue your 4 draws and 3 blows to add meaning and feeling. Now that's the blues!

This 12 bar blues cycle concentrates on the low end of your harp. Two draw is sometimes difficult for beginners. Remember to draw lightly, to pull the air stream towards the top of your head and to push your harp and upper lip up towards your nose.

Evening Star Blues Cycle

I	Riff of Resolution	(1) 2 (2) (2)
IV	Stepping Stone Riff	2 3 2 1
I	Riff of Resolution	(1) 2 (2) (2)
I	Riff of Resolution	(1) 2 (2) (2)
IV	Stepping Stone Riff	(4) (4) (4) 4
IV	Stepping Stone Riff	(4) (4) (4) 4
I	Riff of Resolution	(1) 2 (2) (2)
I	Riff of Resolution	(1) 2 (2) (2)
V	Dominant Wailer	3 (3) 4 (4)
IV	Stepping Stone Riff	(4) (4) (4) 4
I	Riff of Resolution	(1) 2 (2) (2)
V	Dominant Wailer	(1) 2 (2) (3) 4 (4)

Notes

* The framework of blues, rock, country western, reggae, new wave et. al. is the I-IV-V CHORD PROGRESSION.

* When accompanying a guitar or piano, the harp player lets these instruments play the I-IV-V Chord Progression.

* WHEN PLAYING SOLO, the harp player plays riffs, patterns of notes that express the progression.

* The basic idea is to play riffs that end on a Note of Resolution to express the I chord, riffs that end on a Wailing Note to express the V chord, and riffs that end on Stepping Stone Note 1 blow, 4 blow, 7 blow or 10 blow to express the IV chord.

* The I-IV-V blues cycle is NOT CARVED IN CONCRETE. The order of riffs can be changed and one riff can be substituted for another.

* The only set rule is that the harp player establishes a home base.

* As the harp player plays the cycle, he or she can use 3 blow as a Note of Resolution one time, 6 blow or 9 blow the next time. Similarly, one Wailing Note can be exchanged for another, one Stepping Stone for another.

* Learning the progressions in this chapter will enhance your harp playing; but the way they sound, the tempo at which they're played, their overall feeling is up to you.

* A tape cassette lesson playing these cycles is available from the Cross Harp Press.

SEVEN

The Sensuous Harmonica Player

What's it like to bend notes? To make your harmonica laugh, cry, coo and wail? Here, at last, are the unabridged answers. In explicit language, the author takes you deep into the heart and soul of the harmonica, and helps you develop a meaningful relationship with this very sensuous musical instrument.

The Sensuous Instrument

Though rarely described in this way, the harmonica is a sensuous instrument – both in the sounds it makes and in the relationship it has with the person who plays it.

For example, the way a harmonicist plays a single note is similar to a kiss. Lips pucker out to embrace the instrument. Mouth is slightly open. Throat opens itself to the unobstructed passage of air. All movement occurs with gentle firmness and rhythmic sensuality.

Only in the embrace of a sensuous single note can the harmonica communicate the musical feelings the player wants so badly to express. Hands open and close, changing the tone from *ahhhhh* to *oooooo*. Notes bend down and curve upwards to create and resolve tension. Tongue *ta ta ta*'s the fleshy ridge behind the upper teeth. Foot stomps a beat on the floor. Harp slides across moist lips. Riffs tremble out unconsciously as the harp plays the player and the player plays the harp.

Harmonica playing is like dancing. The body responds to its own music. There's no self-criticism, no self-judgment. Though structured in a basic understanding of notes, scales, blows and draws, this dance is freeform and individual. It is a dance of breath, tongue, lips, hands, throat and mouth.

There's no other dance like the one that comes to you naturally. It's your rhythm, your style, your mood. It belongs to you, you and the object of your affections, the harmonica.

116

Breathing—How to Avoid Passing Out When Playing Harp

Playing Cross Harp, the beginning harp player's lungs are often filled to capacity from drawing so much. Here are some tips to help you deal with this problem.

Consider: if you take a QUICK deep breath, you can fill your lungs in about half a second.

On the other hand, if you take a SLOW deep breath you can keep the air streaming into your lungs for 10, 15, 20 or even 30 seconds.

This slow sucking and blowing of air is the way you should meet your body's breathing needs. Watch the second hand of a clock as you play 4 draw. See how long you can make the note last. When your lungs are almost filled, blow on hole 3. Keep the airstream controlled instead of allowing it to explode into your harp. How long can you make the 3 blow last? When your lungs are almost empty, draw on hole 4 again. Then play a long, controlled blow.

Working with this blow and draw exercise will help you gain control over your breathing. Before long, you'll never run out of breath when playing harmonica.

Some additional tips:

* Excess air in the lungs can be released by playing a blow note, or simply by taking the harp away from your mouth and exhaling.

* Breathing needs can also be satisfied by phrasing your riffs. Play the Up Riff to a 4 stomp beat. Take the harp away from your mouth for 4 stomps. Then play the Down Riff to the same four stomp cadence. Remember, silence is an integral part of music.

* When blowing, don't puff your cheeks. Rather, draw your cheeks *in* a little bit to help guide the airstream down the center of your mouth.

The Sensuous Bender

You are playing the Up Riff. Harp is set well between your puckered lips. Upper lip rests comfortably on the upper plate of the harp. To facilitate this, harmonica is tilted slightly down, into your mouth.

With an up and out pucker, you guide a gentle blow into hole 3. Immediately, the airstream reverses itself to coax 3 draw through the reeds. In almost the same motion, you move the harp to hole 4 and blow. Without the slightest hesitation, you draw.

And there you are, wailing on 4 draw, creating musical tension as the sound of your harmonica fills the room.

A large, vibrant airstream channels through the harp, tickling the insides of your puckered lips and narrowed cheeks, splashing against the back of your throat, cascading down into your voice box and lungs.

Now, you hollow out your throat and draw the airstream directly into your voice box. With an almost mirrored response, the 4 draw swoops down, playing the note much lower than usual.

This flattening of the note creates even more tension as your 4 draw Wailer bounces off the walls. The ear that hears this curving tone is pleased and surprised.

Slowly, you release the air pressure from your voice. As the focus of the airstream moves slowly up your throat, the flattened 4 draw bends slowly upwards.

The ear leans forward. What is happening here?

118

Pounding your foot to a 4 stomp beat, you return to 3 blow – but not to resolve tension. No, it's much too soon for that.

You've come back to the 3 blow to play the Up Riff again. Blow-draw on hole 3, blow-draw on hole 4. As you play this fabulous 4 draw Wailing Note, you suck the air deep into your voice box... and release it.

The 4 draw has now played two notes, 4 draw bent and 4 draw unbent. The way the flattened 4 draw slurred up into the unbent 4 draw has pleased and excited the ear. It isn't exactly sure what happened – but it sure felt good.

What next? Appreciating the importance of repetition in music, you play the Up Riff once again. Only this time when you draw on hole 4, you quickly shift the focus of the airstream from throat to voice box, throat to voice box.

Weee ewe weee ewe weee ewe! Your lips wiggle and your throat and mouth hollow out as though whistling these vowel sounds on the inhale.

Naturally, the harp responds perfectly. The *weeee* vowel sound drawn through hole 4 plays an unbent single note.

The *ewe* sound automatically hollows out the throat and changes the shape of the lips. In this position, the airstream curves down to the voice box, and the 4 draw does exactly what the airstream does. It curves down almost a full note.

Immediately, mouth and throat return to the *weee* position, and the air pressure shoots to the top of your throat. The note curves to the top of its bending range.

Ewe. The note dips down. *Weee.* The note bends up.

Weee ewe weee ewe weee ewe!

Four draw wails like this for four beats.

On the fourth beat, the listening ear is now tingling with anticipation. What will you do now?

You rat! You've built all this tension and you've stopped playing.

You're pausing. That's right. You've stopped playing, but your foot keeps right on stomping. The tension of that long, wailing 4 draw hangs in the air. 1-2-1-2 stomps your foot. 1-2-1-2.

Again, you play a quick bending 4 draw going *wee ewe, wee ewe, wee ewe.* Four beats pass. Then, the 4 draw curves down towards the 4 blow. Your breath reverses as the note hits the low part of the bend. Now, you're playing the 4 blow. Without a pause, you move the harp to hole 3 and draw this molasses-thick note into your voice box. The tension is incredible as the 3 draw bends deeper and deeper. You're almost to the Note of Resolution, 3 blow – but not quite.

The ear quivers, "Oh, give it to me! Give me that Note of Resolution!"

"Do you really want it?" the deeply bent 3 draw asks.

"Oh, yes! More than anything!" cries the ear.

The 3 draw bends lower still. Almost to resolution, but still a hair's breadth away.

"Please! Don't tease me. I can't stand it!" cries the frantic ear.
The air pressure in your hollowed-out voice box travels slightly up, then back down. Gently, you blow.

"Ahhhhh," sighs the ear. "Resolution. It feels soooo good." It staggers, almost falling off the head of its owner. Then it says, "That was incredible. Could you do it again. PLEASE?"

The Practical Bender

Dig it. Bending isn't a talent. It's a knack. The first step of acquiring this knack is getting a clear single note with an out and up pucker and the harp deep in your lips.

Once you're playing full single notes, move the focus of your drawn airstream from the back of your throat DOWN into your voice box. This *manipulation* of your airstream is similar to whistling high and then whistling low – except that the whistle is on the draw instead of the blow.*

When you draw a note into your voice box, you hollow out your throat. This hollowing guides the airstream down to the area where you swallow. It feel somewhat like yawning, except that you keep your lips puckered.

Here are some tips for benders:

* Pucker sensuously when you bend.

* Keep the volume of your note constant.

* When bending, do not drop or clench your jaw. Don't grimace, or tighten up.

* Don't wiggle the tip of your tongue.

* Don't play all your notes bent, or there will be no bend, only flat notes. Play notes in both the bent and unbent positions.

---

* On holes 1 through 6, you can bend only the draw notes. On holes 7 through 10, you can bend blow notes.

Bending One Draw and Four Draw

On your **C** harp:
One draw and 4 draw (same notes but an octave apart) are usually easiest to bend. In regular blues playing, 4 draw is played more than 1 draw.

Some basic bends are:

Two Step Bend

Slur your 4 draw bent to 4 draw unbent.

Wailing Bend

Make the 4 draw undulate between high and low by quickly shifting the focus of air pressure from shallow throat to deep throat.

Tongue Bend

Bend the 4 draw down as you tongue triplets. Keep tonguing as you slowly bring the note back up. The result is a rhythmic staccato of curving notes that perfectly blend into each other.

Tongue Wailer Bend

Tongue the high and low spots of the undulating wailing bend. You get a staccato of high, low, high, low, etc.

Fancy Tongue Wailer Bend

Tongue the unbent 4 draw twice and the bent 4 draw once. This is one of an infinite number of variations on the tongue-bend theme.

Some riffs on which to bend or tongue-bend the 4 draw are:

Up Riff
3 ③ 4 ④

Down Riff
④ 4 ③ 3

Six Blow to Four Draw Down
6 ⑤④

Bending Two Draw

As a rule of thumb (or lip), if you are able to get a clear single note on the 2 draw of your **C** harp, you are playing single notes correctly.

On the other hand, if your 2 draw won't respond, your single note technique needs help. Try moving the harp UP towards your nose. Relax your lips, but keep a deep, sensuous pucker. As you draw, direct that airstream to the roof of your mouth. Pull that note UP.

Now, the unbent 2 draw is a Note of Resolution. It's the same note as 3 blow. The advantage of 2 draw is that you can get there quickly from 1 draw and 2 blow – and you can bend 2 draw down an entire note.

The note you bend down to is a Stepping Stone Note. It's essentially the same note as 5 draw, only down an octave. Use this bent 2 draw to create tension and expectation for the unbent 2 draw.

Start by getting a clear single note on 2 draw. Then suck the note down, deep into your voice box. Your 2 draw may distort, but that's okay as long as the note is actually lowering. In fact, a distorted, bent 2 draw is one of the hallmark sounds of blues harp.

When the note pulls down, hold it there. Then gradually allow the bent 2 draw to return to its unbent position.

Two Step Bend

When you are able to bend 2 draw down and back up, try *starting* the bend with the bent 2 draw and slowly bring it up.

Wailing Bend

Try bending 2 draw up and down very quickly. Remember to end the bend on the unbent 2 draw Note of Resolution.

Two Step Tongue Bend

Tongue the note in triplets. The first two syllables should be in the low part of the bend. The third should announce the high part.

The Good Morning Riff is an excellent way to use the bending potential of 2 draw.

Bending Three Draw

To play good blues harp, you need to learn to bend 3 draw just right. There are three possible notes within the 3 draw. The 3 draw unbent is the 3rd note of the 1-3-5 combination of harmonizing notes. Although it will always work when accompanying a I-IV-V chord progression, unbent 3 draw will not sound bluesy. And, if your guitarist is using the seventh chord in his I-IV-V progression, the 3 draw unbent may not work at all.

When you lower the 3 draw by bending, you play the 2½ note of the major scale. This is the blues harmonizing note discovered by Adam.

If you bend the 3 draw even lower, you'll play the 2nd note of the major scale – and this too can sound very bluesy.

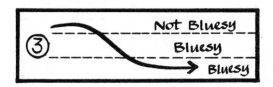

There may be a feeling of resistance in the airstream you draw through hole 3. Somehow this note feels *thicker* than the 4 draw or 6 draw. Once you get used to it, this feeling of thickness can give you amazing control in bending the 3 draw.

Don't force the 3 draw. Coax it. Kiss the harmonica fully and sensuously. Make the airstream large and pull 3 draw down to your guts. Then blow on hole 3. That's the only way to do it.

Establish your Note of Resolution by tonguing the 3 blow. Play 3 draw bent, continuing your tonguing. Then resolve on 3 blow.

Three Draw and Blow Boogie

$$3 \quad ③ \quad 3$$

Q means draw and bend down

Bending Six Draw

Six draw is the same note as the bent 3 draw, except it is an octave higher. Since 6 draw is a Wailing Note, you can tongue and bend it through an entire blues cycle. You can easily resolve the tension created by 6 draw by playing Note of Resolution 6 blow.

Six Draw Wail and Six Blow Resolution

Some effective bends on the 6 draw are:

Two Step Bend

Tongue Bend

Wailing Bend

Riffs that work well with the 6 draw bending are:

Upper Riff
3 ③ 4 ④ ⑥ 6

Play the Up Riff. Wail on 4 draw. Without stopping your draw, slide to 6 draw. Wail and bend to create tension. Resolve on 6 blow.

Nine Blow Down
9 ⑨ 8 ⑧ ⑦⑥ 6

Before resolving on the 6 blow, stretch the 6 draw out, slowly curving it towards the Note of Resolution. When you go from 6 draw to 6 blow, reverse your breath smoothly. Make it seem that the 6 draw has slurred down into the 6 blow.

What About Five Draw?

Playing Cross Harp, 5 draw is a Stepping Stone Note. Then why does it sound so good when you play it by mistake? Five draw is the 6½ note of Adam's Blues Scale. It won't harmonize throughout an entire I-IV-V progression, but when you use it as a Stepping Stone, 5 draw is a great note.

Try the 4 and 5 Draw Slide: quickly swivel your harp between holes 4 and 5. Don't stop your single note draw. This 4 and 5 Draw slide adds a warbling blues sound to your music. Use it to create musical tension.

127

Here's another riff using the 5 draw.

Five Draw Descender
(5) 5 (4) 5 (4) 4 (3) 3

Experiment with your 5 draw. Don't play it too loud, too long, too often: but play it!

Bending Nine Blow

Yes, Virginia, you *can* bend blow notes. But only the high ones. In particular, the Note of Resolution, 9 blow. The idea is to bend it down to create a sense of tension, and to bend it back up to release the tension.

The first step in bending 9 blow is getting a clear single note. Then you push your airstream forward and DOWN into the harmonica. To bring the bend back up, let the focus of air pressure in the harmonica rise. This is easiest on the lower key harps such as **G** or **A**.

Nine blow can be played in a wailing bend:

It can be curved down to slur into the next lowest note, 9 draw. This is especially effective on a riff that heads down such as the 9 Blow Down.

Nine blow can also be curved down and up to blend into 10 blow – a Stepping Stone Note that sounds bluesy when bent.

10	Stepping
(10)	Stepping
9	RESOLUTION

Practice bending your 9 blow in the 6 Blow Up Riff.

Six Blow Up
6 ⑦⑧8 9

Your Hands–
How To Make Your Harp Talk

If you want, your harmonica can be a church organ inside a cathedral. A funky cathedral, true. But would you have it any other way?

The cathedral is your cupped hands. They create an air chamber around your harp. With this air chamber open, your harp says *ahhhhhhhh* on a note such as 3 blow. When your hands close, sealing the chamber around the harp, 3 blow says *oooooooooo* (pronounced *ewe*).

By going from closed to open on 3 blow three times in a row, you can make your harp say *oooooo ahhhhhh oooooooo ahhhhhhhh oooooooo ahhhhhhhhhhh*.

Playing 3 blow with your hands closed and quickly opening them makes the harp say *waaaa*. Doing it twice makes the harp say *waaaa waaaa*.

You can use your hands to shape your tones, giving notes a talking quality. You can also use them to punctuate your music much as you use tonguing to break a long blow or draw into a chain of staccato pieces.

In addition, you can combine the effects your hands create with tonguing and bending. For instance, bending 4 draw down is enhanced when you keep your hands open at the start of the bend, close them as you bring the note down, and open them as you bring the note back up.

The same is true of any note you bend. Closing your hands makes the note deeper. The sealed air chamber gives added control in bending the note. It mellows your tone, sweetens your sound, and adds a new dimension to your harp playing.

Cupping your hands works best on your low notes – holes 1 through 6. This means your cup doesn't have to provide an air chamber for the entire harmonica. Forming your cup to cover only the lower notes will do quite nicely.

There are two basic styles of cups for harp players. One is for small hands. The other is for large hands.

If you have small hands, place the harp between the thumb and forefinger of your left hand. Form an upside-down cup with four fingers of your left hand.

With your right hand, form a cup and place it beneath the harp holding thumb of your left hand. Curve the palm and fingers of your right hand's cup so there is an air chamber beneath the lower four holes of your harp.

To open the cup, swing the right hand down about an inch. Use the connection between the heel of your cupped right hand and your left hand's harp-holding thumb as a hinge. Make this closing and opening motion smooth. You don't have to drop the right hand's palm very far to make the harp say *wa*!

Some additional tips for people using the small hand cupping technique:

* When holding the harp between the thumb and forefinger of your left hand, be sure you're gripping the harp towards the back of the instrument. Otherwise, your fingers will keep you from getting a sensuous pucker for your single note.

* If you can't get a good *waaaa* by closing and opening your hands search for leaks in your cup and rearrange your hands so that the cup is sealed.

* Make the opening and closing movements of your right hand gentle and smooth. This will make your harp playing more graceful. It will also keep you from losing your single note when you move your hands.

* Once you have the basic idea of forming an air chamber, arrange your hands so they feel natural to you.

For people with large hands, there is another cupping technique. Curve your left hand and place it at a 45 degree angle to the floor. Hold the harmonica by sticking its end in the fleshy notch between the heel of your left hand and the thumb. DO NOT use your little finger to help balance the harp.

Cup your right hand and place it over your harp-holding left hand. Help balance the harp by placing it against the first inside knuckle of your right hand.

131

Bring the entire harp and hand apparatus to your puckered lips.
Seal the air chamber beneath the harp by placing the heels of your
hands against both sides of your jaw.

Your right hand can curve around so it practically covers holes
7, 8, 9, 10. When you want to play these holes, pull the hand back
and slide the harp.

As with the small hand method of cupping the harp, the air chamber
is beneath the harmonica. To open the chamber and make your
harp say *wa!*, let your right thumb serve as a hinge for the cupped
right hand. Open the hand and close it. Make the motion smooth,
like dancing.

If your harp's tone isn't responding, look for air leaks. Have you
form-fitted the edges of the heels of your hand to your jaw and chin?
Are your hands relaxed? Have you created an actual pocket out of
your palms and fingers?

Now, get yourself a microphone. Specific kinds are mentioned in Chapter XI. Cup your hands around that mike and your harp. Plug the mike into an amplifier. YOWWWWW! What was that awful screech? It's called feedback. It's what happens when the sound coming out of your amp is picked up by your microphone.

Step away from your amp so the speaker isn't pointed directly at your microphone. Now, blow and draw. Keep your hands airtight. If you have difficulty cupping the mike and harp at the same time, wrap a piece of wetsuit material (also known as neoprene) around the mike to form a tunnel. A rubber band wrapped around the neoprene will make this semi-permanent.

Now cup the harp to the neoprene tunnel. You should have a perfect air chamber leading directly into your microphrone. The flexibility of the neoprene will feel great on your fingers.

Adjust the tone of the amp to accentuate the low sounds. Give yourself lots of volume. Sounds great, but can you turn it up a little? They can't hear you down the street.

With the help of these instructions, find a way of holding and cupping the harmonica that feels good to you. Everyone's hands are a little different, and it follows that everyone cups the harmonica a little bit differently. Think of your hands as dancers, sensuous creatures who love music. Trust them to find a way of making that harp talk.

Notes

* The most important skill in harp playing is being able to get a clear, rich SINGLE note.

* To keep from running out of breath when playing harp, learn the trick of the SLOW INHALE.

* BENDING is a technique in which the harp player lowers the note by manipulating the airstream, pulling it DOWN into the lungs.

* Bending is very difficult if you don't have a good single note with an up and out pucker of your lips. It's not difficult when your single note technique is correct.

* Bending helps the harp player create tension. Below hole 6, bend 1 draw, 2 draw, 3 draw, 4 draw and 6 draw. Above hole 6, bend 8 draw, 9 blow and 10 blow.

* Bending can be combined with TONGUING.

* CUPPING your hands around the harp mellows tone and makes the harp say *oooooooo*. Opening your hands makes the harp say *ahhhhhhhh*.

* Use the instructions on hands to find the way of cupping the harp that feels best to you. Everybody's hands are different, and each harp player's cup is a little different.

EIGHT

Stone Goes Straight

Straight Harp is the style of harmonica that sounds best with ballads and jazz. More melodic than Cross Harp, it's also easier to play. In Chapter VIII, Stone goes straight, brings a woman vocalist to practice and the band tunes up.

The Mysterious Visitor

One Sunday afternoon Stone showed up for practice in a suit and tie.

"Hey!" demanded Smash. "What's going on here?"

Before Stone could answer, a woman stepped into the entrance of the cave. She was tall, slender, and most important to the chauvinist Cave Boys, good-looking.

"Guys," said Stone, "I'd like you to meet a friend of mine. This is Umm."

Six Cave Boy eyes went from Stone to Umm and back to Stone. True, Umm was a dish. But what was this "friend" stuff? If you wanted a woman, you grabbed her by the hair and dragged her back to the cave. You didn't call her "friend." And you sure didn't start wearing a suit and tie.

"Well, do come in," said Krok, nervously fingering his guitar.

"Would you like something to drink?" stammered Smash. "Iced tea maybe?"

Behind her rose-tinted monogrammed "U" glasses, Umm's eyes smiled. The way her hair frizzed out, it looked as though grabbing this lady for a one-night cave encounter would only produce a handful of hairspray.

Umm placed a cigarette in the end of a long, mammoth tusk cigarette holder and lit up. "No thanks," she said to Smash.

"Umm came to hear us play," said Stone.

"I can dig that," said Smash, "But what's with the suit and tie?"

"Listen man," said Stone, "It takes more than grime and sweat to make good music. Let's add a little class to the act. Besides, Umm here has got us a gig."

"A gig?" said Krok, "Where?"

Not exactly a gig – an audition," said Umm.
"What's an addition?" asked Smash.
"It's a gig..." offered Stone.
"But you don't get paid," added Gref.
"If they like you, they ask you to come back," said Krok.
"Then they pay you," chimed Stone.

Smash frowned and rubbed his stubby chin. His drumsticks looked like twigs in his huge hands.

"Where is this audition?" asked Krok.

"At The Club," said Umm, "I know the guy who runs the place."

"Let's practice," Stone said. He loosened his necktie. "I gotta new harp style I want to try. If we're gonna audition, we want to be ready. And look..." he turned to Krok, "this time let's tune up before we play."

"Tune up again?" asked Krok with a shudder. He usually tuned the deer sinew guitar strings about every six months. "What the devil for?"

"So it sounds like we're playing in the same key!" shouted Stone. So an **E** note on your guitar and Gref's bass is the same as an **E** note on my harmonica. So the music doesn't sound like a bunch of Neanderthals banging on pots and pans!"

Krok looked carefully at Stone standing there with his hands on his hips; his suit, loosened tie and "friend" giving him a new air of authority.

Tune up? he thought. It had never made any difference before. It was obvious Stone was just trying to impress this frizz-haired Umm sitting over there in a cloud of cigarette smoke. As leader, songwriter and guitarist for the Cave Boys, Krok considered telling Stone to start walking.
But he stopped himself. Good harp players were hard to find. Besides, if he got rid of Stone, he might lose his audition.

"Okay," he finally said to Stone, "Give me a note."

Tuning Guitars To Harmonicas

On those rare occasions when they did tune, the band always matched notes with Stone's harmonica. It was the only instrument around that didn't change pitch. Bass and guitar strings (especially guitar) got out of tune just sitting around. Hot weather made the strings stretch and get lower. Cold weather made them tighten and get higher.

But when it came to being on key, Stone's harmonica was Old Faithful.

Now, being in tune meant that a certain note on one instrument was the same note on another instrument. The procedure was for Stone to play a note on his harp and for Gref and Krok to tune their instruments to that note.

The guitar strings were set up like this. The first string was tuned to an **E** note. The second one to a **B**, the third to a **G**, the fourth to a **D**, the fifth to an **A**, and the sixth string to an **E**.

Here's how the guitar looked:

And the bass, a four-stringed instrument, was set up like Krok's guitar. The only difference was that the strings were much thicker and were set down an octave from the guitar.

So, on both bass and guitar, the lowest string needed to be tuned to an **E** note. Stone pulled out his **C** harp. The layout of notes looked like this:

"Gimme an **E**, a low **E**," said Gref.

Stone played a 2 blow on his **C** harp. Bass and guitar strings varoomed as the **E** strings were tightened to play the same note as an **E** on Stone's harmonica.

"Okay, gimme an **A**," said Krok, once his **E** string was in tune.

Stone played a 6 draw, careful not to bend it so Krok and Gref would not be tuning to a flattened note.

Again, bass and guitar strings twanged.

Smash sighed impatiently. Tuning was necessary, he guessed. But it took so long! Why couldn't the band just play and pretend they were in tune?

"How 'bout a **D**?" asked Gref once the **E** and **A** strings on the guitar and bass were the same pitch as the **E** and **A** notes on the harp.

Again careful not to bend the note or cup the harp in his hands, Stone now played a 4 draw on his **C** harp. This was his **D** note.

For the **G** strings, Stone played a 3 blow. Gref was now tuned. His bass had only four strings. But Krok needed a **B** note.

Stone played an unbent 3 draw.

"Varooom!" went the **B** string as it sought out the pitch that would match Stone's **B**.

And for the final note, another **E**, Stone played a higher **E** on his harp: the 5 blow.

Krok carefully tightened the tuning peg and his high **E** string slid up towards the same pitch as the harp's **E** note.

Finally, the two sounds were the same.

Krok strummed a **C** chord. Gref played a riff on the 1-3-5 harmonizing notes of the **C** scale. Stone played a **C** note, the 4 blow on his **C** harp. Even though he didn't need to tune, Smash banged his drums.

"Guess we're there," said Krok.

"Your **B** string is a little flat," said Umm.

"My what?" Krok could not believe he was hearing this.

"Your **B** string," said Umm, smiling sweetly from her cloud of smoke. "Go ahead, strum your **C** chord again. You'll hear it."

Krok strummed each string on his **C** chord. Sure enough, the **B** did sound slightly out of whack. He tightened the tuning peg.

'Mmmmmmmmmmmm," he said to Umm. "Not only pretty, but smart, too."

"Why don't you guys play something?" she quietly asked.

"Yeah..." said Smash. He brought his sticks down on his snare drums with a tremendous bang.

Stone Jams Straight Harp

"Okay," said Krok, "Let's try that slow love song, 'Cave Angel.' It would go over real good at The Club. Key of **C**. Slow tempo. Guess you'll count up four steps from the **C** and play Cross Harp on an **F** harmonica," he said to Stone.

Stone smiled quietly. "No, I'm gonna do something different on this song. I'm gonna play my **C** harp in the key of **C**. You know... Straight Harp. It sounds more...more..."

"Romantic..." said Umm.

"Yeah, romantic."

Krok squinted at his harp player. Romantic? What had this woman done to him?

"Okay. Here goes," he finally said, "One, two, one, two, three, four..."

Krok strummed the I chord of "Cave Angel." This was, of course, a **C** chord. Gref added supporting notes on his bass, and Smash played a soft steady rhythm.

Then Krok played an **A** minor chord, the relative minor of the **C** chord. From here the music went into an **F** chord, the IV chord of the progression, then it moved to a **G**, the V chord, and returned to the **C**, the I Chord of Resolution.

Using the relative minor chord, the chord 6 steps up the scale from I chord, gave the music a more melodic feeling than did the simple I-IV-V progression. Now the progression went I-VI-IV-V. Although this occurred thousands of years ago, Krok's music sounded remarkably like one of those slow-dance pop ballads that were so popular in the late 1950's and early 60's.

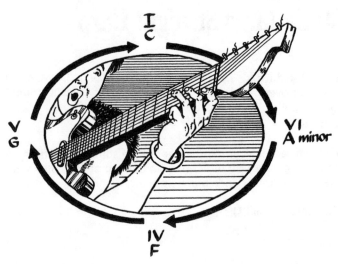

Krok began to sing:

>   C   Am   F   G
> **"Cave angel, what can I do?**
>   C   Am   F   G
> **To earn your love so true?**
>   C   Am   F   G   C
> **Cave angel, will you be mine?"**

Umm leaned forward. These guys might look rowdy, but they weren't half bad. The blood began to flow more quickly through her heart.

Meanwhile, Stone was preparing to enter the music. He held his **C** harp to his puckered lips.

He hadn't played Straight Harp with the band before. Normally, he used this harp style for playing melodies around a campfire. He couldn't get down and boogie playing Straight Harp. He couldn't get that bluesy, tension-creating feeling.

Still, on this slow moving, pretty love song, bluesy Cross Harp would be out of place. So Straight Harp it was.

144

Straight Harp Revisited

This is the way Straight Harp works (from a Cave Boy's point of view). Take your **C** harmonica and blow on holes 1234. This is your Straight Harp Blow Chord.

You can also play the Straight Harp Blow Chord by playing holes 4567 blow or 789 and 10 blow. ALL your blow notes are harmonizing notes.

The Notes of Resolution are 1 blow, 4 blow, 7 blow and 10 blow.

The basic approach, then, to playing improvisational Straight Harp is to accent the blow notes, use the draw notes as Stepping Stones (almost the exact opposite of Cross Harp) and to resolve on 1 blow, 4 blow, 7 blow or 10 blow.

Map of Straight Harp

	10	RESOLUTION
	⑩	Stepping Stone
	9	WAILING
	⑨	Stepping Stone
	8	WAILING
	⑧	Stepping Stone
	7	RESOLUTION
	⑦	Stepping Stone
	⑥	Stepping Stone
	6	WAILING
	⑤	Stepping Stone
	5	WAILING
	④	Stepping Stone
	4	RESOLUTION
	③	Stepping Stone
	3	WAILING
	②	WAILING
	2	WAILING
	①	Stepping Stone
	1	RESOLUTION

THE STRAIGHT HARP I CHORD OF RESOLUTION is expressed with single notes 1 blow, 4 blow, 7 blow and 10 blow.

THE IV STEPPING STONE CHORD is expressed with single notes 5 draw, 9 draw and 2 draw bent down.

THE DOMINANT WAILER V CHORD is expressed with single notes 2 draw, 3 blow, 6 blow and 9 blow.

146

As you play Straight Harp, you'll discover that the draw notes – although they're called Stepping Stone Notes – *almost* harmonize. Stepping Stone Notes like 1 draw, 4 draw and 6 draw can be drawn out, accented, as long as a Note of Resolution follows them, or as long as the song isn't on the I chord of the I-IV-V progression.

So, if you're getting clear, single notes, it's pretty hard to make a mistake playing Straight Harp.

Here's a simple Straight Harp Riff that will always harmonize if you are in tune with the guitarist and are playing the right key of harmonica.

Meadow Lark Melody Run
5 ④ 4

You can also play the Meadow Lark Melody Run on the high and low end of your harmonica.

High Meadow Lark Melody Run
8 ⑧ 7

Low Meadow Lark Melody Run
2 ① 1

You can play an Up and Down Meadow Lark Melody Run by returning to the Straight Harp Wailing Note 5 blow immediately after playing the 4 blow.

Up and Down
Meadow Lark Melody Run
5 ④ 4 5 5 ④ 4

High Up and Down
Meadow Lark Melody Run
8 ⑧ 7 8 8 ⑧ 7

As mentioned earlier, Straight Harp does not create a bluesy wailing tension in the manner of Cross Harp. And, beneath 7 blow, the blow notes can't be bent.

However, on hole 7 and above, the blow notes *can* be bent. By pushing the airstream forward and down, you can make your 7 blow, 8 blow, 9 blow and 10 blow swoop down. And, by releasing the air you've directed down into your harmonica, you can bring these Straight Harp Harmonizing Notes back to the top of their bending potentials.

For instance, you can create tension on the High Meadow Lark Melody Run by bending the 8 blow Wailing Note.

And, you can resolve the tension with the Straight Harp Descender, a pattern that takes you from Straight Harp Wailing Note 8 blow down to Straight Harp Note of Resolution 4 blow.

Straight Harp Descender
8 (8) 7 (6) 6 5 4

From the 4 blow, you can wind your way to the Wailing Note 8 blow.

Straight Harp Ascender
4 ④ 5 6 7 ⑧ 8

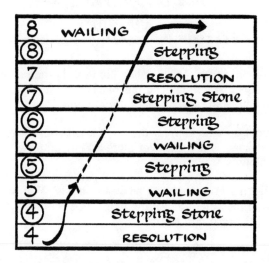

These patterns should give you a few ideas for Straight Harp improvisational accompaniment. You can use them as "fillers" – musical phrases that keep a song interesting, or you can use them to create solos. Built on a framework of Straight Harp Harmonizing Notes, the mood and timing of these riffs can be modified to fit the song you're accompanying.

In addition, you can figure out almost all melodies that use a major scale and play them in the Straight Harp Style. The only major scale on your diatonic harp starts on 4 blow and goes:

4 ④ 5 ⑤ 6 ⑥ ⑦ 7
do re mi fa so la ti do

So if your band were going to release a new version of "Old Mac-
Donald Had A Farm," you, the harp player, could toot around on
this major scale until you discovered the melody.

7   7   7   6   ⑥ ⑥ 6
Old MacDonald had a farm

8   8   ⑧   ⑧   7
Eeeeeyyyy eeeeeyyyy ohhhh

But say the record producer didn't like the way the harp sounded.
"C'mon," he says, "You're making this MacDonald guy sound like a
pansy. How 'bout some lower, more throaty notes?"

Then you might go searching for the melody on your lower notes –
and to your dismay, you'd discover there isn't a complete scale from
1 blow to 4 blow.

You'd find that the *fa* was missing as well as the *la*. You would
NOT be able to play the note for the word "had" in those poignant
lines, "Old MacDonald had a farm."

4   4   3   ?   3
Old Mac Donald had a farm

Panic sets in! Here you are on the verge of a big recording contract
– and you can't find the note for "had."

What you need is a major scale from 1 blow to 4 blow. Okay. Here's
what you do. There are notes missing between 2 blow and 2 draw
and between 3 blow and 3 draw.

The only way to play a major scale is to bend to 2 draw down before
playing the unbent 2 draw, and to bend the 3 draw down before
playing the unbent 3 draw.

1   ①   2   ②   ②③ ③ 4
do re mi fa so la ti do

Q   means draw and bend down

150

The note you'd need for playing the "had" in "Old MacDonald" would be the 3 draw bent down.

4 4 3 ③̬ 3
Old MacDonald had a farm
5 5 ④ ④ 4
Eeeeeyyyy eeeeeyyyy ohhh

"Perfect!" cries the producer. "You're going to go a long ways with this little tune!"

So, to enhance your ability in playing Straight Harp melodies, practice this major scale starting from 1 blow.

1 ① 2 ②̬ ②③̬③ 4
do re mi fa so la ti do

And also learn to play the major scale going from 4 blow to 1 blow.

4 ③ ③̬ ② ②̬ 2 ① 1
do ti la so fa mi re do

This may be the most difficult technique in the entire book. Still, when "Old MacDonald" strikes it big and your group has started a whole new musical genre, "Punk Nursery Rhymes," don't forget where you learned it.

~~~

But let's get back to Stone, standing there in the musty cave, sweating like Niagara in his suit and loosened tie, **C** harp to his lips as the Cave Boys enter another cycle of this old *be bop* chord progression.

Stone tongues his 4 blow. He slides the harp to 5 blow and plays the Meadow Lark Melody Run: 5 blow, 4 draw, 4 blow. He wails on the 8 blow, slips up to the 9 blow and wails there. Back to the 8 blow, bending the note and releasing it. Then the 8 Blow Descender – 8 blow, 8 draw, 7 blow, 6 draw, 6 blow, 5 blow, 4 blow – hitting that

Straight Harp Note of Resolution at exactly the moment the chord progression has gone full cycle and resolves on the I chord.

It sounds so good, Krok almost drops his guitar. His monkey suited harpist has created a spell with his sensitive Straight Harp. Krok closes his eyes and begins to sing.

"I'd take a bath, I'd comb my hair." A soft 8 blow reverberates off the cave walls. "To show you how much I care." The 8 blow curves down and seems to fall through space as Stone plays the 8 Draw Descender. "Cave angel, will you be mine?" The harmonica echoes the voice with the Meadow Lark Melody run. *Wa wa wa!* the 4 blow actually cries.

"Cave angel...." *Wa wa wa*
"Cave angel...." *Wa wa wa*
"Cave angel...." *Wa wa wa*
"Cave angel...." Only this time the voice doesn't belong to Krok. No, Krok's voice is halfway between a belch and a grunt. This voice is rich, expressive. It belongs to Umm. She's standing up, hands clenched to her bosom, eyes closed, mouth open.

"Cave angel, will you be mine?"

The entire cave seems to be swinging back and forth to this sad, gut wrenching melody. Umm's voice is like a musical instrument. The harp punctuates the music, underscores the emotion. Smash keeps a steady beat. Gref's bass is supportive, sensitive.

Finally, the song ends. The musicians are exhausted, but amazed. This girl can sing! Smash is the first to speak.

"Wow! A chick singer!"

Umm glares, "A woman vocalist."

"Well, guys?" Stone asks, "Can she join our band?"

"We couldn't call ourselves the Cave Boys," says Gref.

"Yeah," says Smash, "It would seem funny."

152

Umm looks at the four musicians. These guys weren't bad. And they were nice enough. Dumb, true. But at least they got into the music. Should she? Well, why not?

"I've got an idea," she says, "How 'bout Umm and the Cave Boys?"

"Sounds good to me," grins Stone.

"I like it," says Gref. "What do you think, Krok?"

All eyes turn to guitarist, songwriter and lead singer of the band. "Well, what do you think?"

No answer. But in Krok's mind, the possibilities are spinning like peaches and cherries on a slot machine. First, they get the job at The Club. Then they move on, playing Dinosaur Breath a couple of nights a week (it's a nice little dive near the tar pits), and then maybe to the big time. Money, booze, women...and maybe, just maybe, Umm, too.

He eyes the frizzy-haired phenomenon standing across the cave. Firelight flickers in her hair, sparkles in her "U" monogrammed glasses, throws shadows on her high, delicate cheekbones.

"Well, tell me this," he says, "How are you at singing rock and blues?"

With that Umm opens her mouth and shouts-sings-laughs-cries, "Baby, why you treat me like you do? Whyyyy? Whyyyy? Whyyyy?"

"Oh yeah!" grunts the voice in Krok's head. "Oh yeah!"

He can see it now. Las Vegas. New York. Los Angeles. World tours. Cosmic tours. Records. Royalties. Revenge on all the people who said he'd never make it. And all because of Umm, this sweet little chick singer, Umm.

"Well," he finally says, "Your voice needs work, but I'll spend some extra time working with you."

"Whooopppppppeeeeeee!" shouts Smash.

And that is how Stone's Straight Harp added diversity and class to a ragged old band that never would have made it out of the cave.

"Incidentally," said Umm, "I think your **B** string is still a little flat."

Notes

* Two instruments that aren't tuned to each other sound lousy when played at the same time.

* Being IN TUNE means that an **E** note on the guitar is the same as an **E** note on a harp. Ditto for **A, D, G, B** or any other note.

* The guitar tunes to the harmonica. The harp player gives the guitarist a note and tells him or her what note it is. On an **E** harp, 1 blow is an **E**. On a **D** harp, 1 blow is a **D**. On a **G** harp, 1 blow is a **G**.

* On your **C** harmonica, 2 blow and 5 blow are **E** notes. Use the major scale chart on page 141 to figure out where other important guitar tuning notes are located.

* To play the Straight Harp style of harmonica, play a **C** harp in the key of **C**, a **G** harp in the key of **G**, a **D** harp in the key of **D**. Accent the blow notes. Use draw notes as Stepping Stones.

* Playing Straight Harp, the Notes of Resolution are 1 blow, 4 blow, 7 blow and 10 blow.

NINE

Campfire Melodies

Umm, Stone, Krok, Gref and Smash vacation in the mountains and Stone plays a number of songs that sound best when the stars are twinkling and the campfire is burning.

A Circle of Friends

The vacationing band sat around the campfire. The descent of the sun had turned the horizon from blue to purple, and the first stars of the evening were taking a bow in a theatre of clear skies.

Krok threw a log on the fire and a shower of sparks made everyone move. Umm told a joke about smoke keeping away the mosquitos. The laughter and talk drifted into a contented silence. Only the fire seemed lively, snapping and crackling, drawing all eyes into a kaleidoscope of blue and orange warmth.

As the sky darkened, Stone and his friends leaned closer to the glowing logs. The harp man took his harmonica from his pocket and started to softly play.

"Wa wa wa waaaaaa!"

His simple Cross Harp riffs kept beat to the crackling of flame and wood. A jug of wine made its way around the fire, passed hand to hand, hand to mouth.

"Wa wa wa waaaaaa!" sang the harp.
"Wa wa oooooo ahhhh!"

Krok placed some dry wood on the fire and Stone's harmonica
energy rose with the flame. So did the energy of his circle of friends.
Smash grunted "Amen" after a particularly soulful phrase. "Yeah!"
said Gref.

The party had started. The fire danced to the singing harmonica,
cracking and popping a fiesty percussion; castanets on fingers of
flame. The wine made its sloshing way around the fire once more.
Stone brought his music to a close.

"Alright!" said a shadowy face across the fire. It was Umm. "Play
some more," she urged. "Play something we can all sing."

"Yeah!" said Smash, carried away by the beauty of the moment.
"Play, uh...'Tom Dooley.' You know, that ol' cowboy song. Everybody knows it."

"Play 'I Been Working On The Railroad,'" said Gref.

"Play 'Froggie Went A' Courtin'" giggled Umm.

"Well, okay," said Stone, "but only if you'll sing along."

Shyly, at first, Stone started to play. The cracked voices of Gref and
Smash were matched by Umm's higher harmony. Even Krok, who
was often embarrassed by innocence and fun, began singing along in
his rough-hewn blues voice. Then he even grabbed his backpacking
guitar and began strumming chords.

To tell the truth, it didn't sound that great – not for the best rock and
blues band in the prehistoric world. But what the hell, they were on
vacation, and having a good time.

And, as Umm said, "There's more to life than the blues."

Now, as the fire dances and the band sings alone, you should try a
few of the following campfire melodies. The songs are presented to
help you learn more about the harmonica, and add to your own
campfire repertoire.

Skip To My Lou

5   *4*   *5*   *6*

Skip, skip, skip to my Lou

④   ③   ④   ⑤

Skip, skip, skip to my Lou

5   *4*   *5*   *6*

Skip, skip, skip to my Lou

④ *5* ⑤ *5* ④ *4*

Skip to my Lou, my darlin'

Skip To My Lou

8   *7*   *8*   *9*

Skip, skip, skip to my Lou

⑧   ⑦   ⑧   ⑨

Skip, skip, skip to my Lou

8   *7*   *8*   *9*

Skip, skip, skip to my Lou

⑧ *8* ⑨ *8* ⑧ *7*

Skip to my Lou, my darlin'

160

Tom Dooley

①   2   ②   ③
Hang down your head Tom Dooley

①   2   ②   ③↙
Hang down your head and cry

①   2   ②   ③↙
Hang down your head Tom Dooley

③↙   3   2   3
Poor boy you're going to die

Tom Dooley   Straight Harp

6   ⑥   7   8
Hang down your head Tom Dooley

6   ⑥   7   ⑧
Hang down your head and cry

6   ⑥   7   ⑧
Hang down your head Tom Dooley

⑧   7   ⑥ 7
Poor boy you're going to die

Froggie Went A'Courtin' Cross Harp

3   ③ 3 2 ①② 2 ②

Froggie went a'courtin' and he did ride ahum ahum

③   ④   5 ④ ③ ④   ④

Froggie went a'courtin' and he did ride ahum ahum

③   ④   5 ④ ③

Froggie went a'courtin' and he did ride

3   ③ 3 2 ①② 2 ②

Sword and pistol by his side ahum ahum

Froggie Went A'Courtin' Straight Harp

7   8 7 ⑥ 6 7 ⑥ 7

Froggie went a'courtin' and he did ride ahum ahum

8   9   ⑩ 9 8 9   9

Froggie went a'courtin' and he did ride ahum ahum

8 9   ⑩ 9 8

Froggie went a'courtin' and he did ride

7   8 7 ⑥ 6 7 ⑥ 7

Sword and pistol by his side ahum ahum

162

Streets Of Laredo   Cross Harp

①②   ③↘   ③   ③3②①
As I walked out in the streets of Lardeo

①②   ③↘ ③③↘ 3 ③↘
As I walked out in Laredo one day

④   4 ③ 4 ③ ③↘③   ③↘ 3 ②①
I spied a young cowboy all wrapped in white linen

① ②   ③↘③ ③↘③ 4   ③ ② ③↘ 3
All wrapped in white linen, and as cold as the clay

Streets Of Laredo   Straight Harp

3 4   ④   5   ④4③ 3
As I walked out in the streets of Lardeo

3 4   ④   5④ 4 ④
As I walked out in Laredo one day

6   ⑤ 5 ⑤ 5 ④ 5   ④ 4 ③ 3
I spied a young cowboy all wrapped in white linen

3 4   ④ 5 ④5 ⑤   5 4④ 4
All wrapped in white linen, and as cold as the clay

163

She'll Be Coming 'Round the Mountain   Cross Harp

① 2②   2 ①   2 ②
She'll be coming 'round the mountain when she comes

2 ③③   ④ ③ ③↘ 3 ③↘
She'll be coming 'round the mountain when she comes

④ 4 ③   ③↘ 3
She'll be coming 'round the mountain

3   2   ③↘ 3
She'll be coming 'round the mountain

①   ③ ③↘ 3 ②↘ ②
She'll be coming 'round the mountain when she comes

She'll Be Coming 'Round the Mountain   Straight Harp

6 ⑥ 7   ⑥ 6 5 6 7
She'll be coming 'round the mountain when she comes

7 ⑧ 8   9 8 ⑧ 7 ⑧
She'll be coming 'round the mountain when she comes

9 ⑨ 8   ⑧ 7
She'll be coming 'round the mountain

7   ⑥   ⑧ 7
She'll be coming 'round the mountain

6   8 ⑧ 7 ⑦ 7
She'll be coming 'round the mountain when she comes

164

Pop Goes The Weasel

Cross Harp

②　③　　　③④③　②
All around the cobbler's bench

①　②　　③↴　　③②
The monkey chased the weasel

①　②　　③↴　　③④③②
The monkey thought was all in fun

5　③↴　4　③③
Pop! goes the weasel

Pop Goes The Weasel

Straight Harp

4　④　　　5 6 5 4
All around the cobbler's bench

3　4　　④　　　5 4
The monkey chased the weasel

3　4　　④　　　5 65 4
The monkey thought was all in fun

⑥　④　⑤　5 4
Pop! goes the weasel

Pop Goes The Weasel   Straight Harp High End

7 ⑧   ♭9♭ 7
All around the cobbler's bench
6 7   ⑧   ♭ 7
The monkey chased the weasel
6 7   ⑧   ♭ 9♭ 7
The monkey thought was all in fun
⑩ ⑧ ⑨ ♭ 7
Pop! goes the weasel

Ol' Grey Mare   Straight Harp High End

6 7   ⑧ ♭   ⑧ ♭ ⑧ 7
The ol' grey mare, she ain't what she used to be
⑧   7 ⑧ 7 ⑥ ♭   ⑧ ♭ ⑧ 7
Ain't what she used to be, ain't what she used to be
6 7   ⑧ ♭   ⑧ ♭ ⑧ 7
The ol' grey mare, she ain't what she used to be
⑧   ♭ ⑧ 7
Many long years ago

166

Ol' Grey Mare

① ②   ③↘③   ③↘③ ③↘3

The ol' grey mare, she ain't what she used to be

③↘   3 ③↘ 3 ②↘③   ③↘③ ③↘3

Ain't what she used to be, ain't what she used to be

① ②   ③↘③   ③③ ③↘3

The ol' grey mare, she ain't what she used to be

③↘   ③ ③↘3

Many long years ago

Ol' Grey Mare

3 4   ④ 5   ④ 5 ④4

The ol' grey mare, she ain't what she used to be

④   4 ④ 4 ③ 5   ④ 5 ④4

Ain't what she used to be, ain't what she used to be

3 4   ④ 5   ④ 5 ④4

The ol' grey mare, she ain't what she used to be

④   5 ④4

Many long years ago

TEN

Slant Harp: A Big Time Harp Style

Slant Harp is the style of harmonica many harpists use to accompany songs in Minor Keys. Most appropriate for blues and rock, Slant Harp uses 4 draw as a Note of Resolution.

In Chapter X, Stone makes a television appearance, discovers the secrets of Slant Harp, and finally understands the purpose of musical artistry.

Stone Looks For
A New Harp Style

"There has to be a way. There has to be..." Stone was walking down the mountainside, muttering to himself. His feet slipped on the trailside rocks, and once he even ran into a tree, but the harp-playing Cave Boy barely noticed his own clumsiness. He was bummed.

This had never happened to Stone before. He had ALWAYS been able to provide great accompaniment to any song Umm and the Cave Boys played.

But Krok's new tune, a reggae-flavored ditty called "Volcano Mouth," was giving him trouble. The song was in the key of **A** minor, and for some reason, neither Cross nor Straight Harp sounded very good.

Making matters worse, today was the day of the television appearance. The Cave Boys were scheduled to play on the Dinah Sledgehammer Show, and Krok wanted to introduce "Volcano Mouth" to the fans.

"Listen," he had said to Stone. "If you can't figure out what to play, then don't. No harmonica sounds better than lousy harmonica." Krok had put his arm protectively around Umm's shoulder. "Besides, you wouldn't want to do anything to harm Umm's career, would you?"

"Oh, c'mon," Umm had said, wriggling away from Krok. "It doesn't sound *that bad.*"

Doesn't sound that bad, Stone had repeated to himself. *Doesn't sound that bad.* The purpose of his playing was to sound great. No one had ever said *doesn't sound that bad* about his harp-playing before.

"Hey!" he had sputtered, "I'll figure out something. Ol' Harp Boy Stone can play anything." His nervous laugh had been cut off by Krok's abrupt remark. "Why not just bang a tambourine? We've got harmonica on too many songs already."

170

Now, walking down the mountain trail to the theatre where the show was to be held, Stone brooded over his problem. Playing songs in minor keys had never troubled him before. A minor chord was only a slight variation of a major chord.

Instead of playing the 1st, 3rd and 5th notes of a major scale to form a major chord, what Krok did was strum the 1st, 2½nd and 5th notes of the major scale. This resulted in a minor chord.

To accompany, Stone would ask what key the song was in. If Krok answered, "**A** minor," Stone would count four steps up the scale from **A** (including the **A**)...

A B C D
1 2 3 4

And play Cross Harp on a **D** harmonica. It had always worked before.

Another approach was to play Straight Harp. If the song were in the key of **A** minor, he would count up 3 steps to figure out that **A** minor was the relative minor of the **C** chord. He would then play Straight Harp on a **C** harmonica.

A   B   C
1   2   3

If the song were in **D** minor, he'd count up 3 steps and play an **F** harmonica in the Straight Harp style.

D   E   F
1   2   3

But on "Volcano Mouth" neither Straight nor Cross Harp were worth beans. They didn't follow the tune. It sounded as though he were trying to wedge riffs into spots where they didn't belong. What was he going to do?

Now, with the rock facade of the theatre clearly in sight, Stone's mind started working with desperate energy. What he needed was a new harp style. All the styles he had learned so far were based on the locations of the Notes of Resolution.

For instance, playing Cross Harp, the Notes of Resolution were 2 draw, 3 blow, 6 blow, 9 blow, and, of course, the Cross Harp Draw Chord, holes 1234 drawn at the same time. Blowing Straight Harp, the Notes of Resolution were 1 blow, 4 blow, 7 blow, 10 blow and holes 1234 blown at the same time. Hmmm, he thought, Maybe... just maybe...

Stone placed his **G** harp to his puckered lips and played a 4 draw. Then he played 5 blow, 5 draw, and back to 4 draw. "That's it!" he said aloud. "That's it! USE 4 DRAW AS A NOTE OF RESOLU-TION."

His heart beating to the joyous rhythm of making a new discovery, Stone walked around the back of the theatre and sat himself down near some garbage cans. For the next hour, the Cave Boy harmoni-cist sat there and learned as much as he could about this new harp style – the style he would call SLANT HARP.

172

The Slant Harp Approach

Slant Harp is a rock and blues style that gives riffs and solos a slightly different feeling than Cross or Straight Harp. It creates a sound that is partly bluesy, partly melodic. It creates a MINOR KEY FEELING.

The Slant Harp Formula is to play a harp in the key that is two steps down the scale from the key the guitarist is playing in. For instance, if the guitarist is playing in the key of **E** minor, count back two steps (including the **E**), and play a **D** harp.

A B C D E F G
2 1

And if the song is in the key of **A** minor, count back two steps from the **A**, and play a **G** harp.

D E F G A B C
2 1

This formula, of course, holds true for any minor key the guitarist chooses to play in.

Once playing the correct key of harmonica, all the Slant Harpist has to do is play riffs and patterns that use 1 draw, 4 draw and 8 draw as Notes of Resolution.

Slant Harp Notes of Resolution
1 Draw, 4 Draw, 8 Draw

The Slant Harp Wailing Notes are harmonizing notes that will not make a mistake at any point in the minor key variation of the I-IV-V chord progression.

Slant Harp Wailing Notes
5 Draw, 6 Draw, 9 Draw, 10 Draw

Usually, Stepping Stone Notes can be used as rungs on ladders between one harmonizing note and another. But playing Slant Harp, there are three Stepping Stone Notes that will clash with the music no matter how brief a time they are played. These notes to avoid are 2 draw, 3 blow and 3 draw.

The advanced Slant Harpist can bend 2 draw and 3 draw, and turn them into Wailing Notes. However, as mentioned earlier the beginner should stick to holes 4 draw and above. Because Slant Harp is played on the high end of the harp, it's good to start out on the lower-keyed harmonicas such as **G, A, B** or **C**.

The following page presents a Slant Harp Map showing where Wailing Notes, Notes of Resolution and Stepping Stone Notes are located.

Map of Slant Harp

10	Stepping Stone
(10)	WAILING
9	Stepping Stone
(9)	WAILING
8	Stepping Stone
(8)	RESOLUTION
7	Stepping Stone
(7)	Stepping Stone
(6)	WAILING
6	Stepping Stone
(5)	WAILING
5	Stepping Stone
(4)	RESOLUTION
4	Stepping Stone
(3)	Stepping Stone (avoid)
3	Stepping Stone (avoid)
(2)	Stepping Stone (avoid)
2	Stepping Stone
(1)	RESOLUTION
1	Stepping Stone

With the exception of 1 draw, all Slant Harp harmonizing notes are on 4 draw or above. For this reason, Slant Harp is usually played on the upper end of the harmonica – between 4 draw and 10 draw.

Slant Harp Riffs

As Stone sat near the garbage cans furiously trying to discover the secrets of Slant Harp, a group of children approached.

"Hey!" one of them cried, "It's Stone, the harp player."

The single voice soon turned into a chorus. "It's Stone. It's Stone!" Then the girls and boys crowded aroung the hurried harp player. "What's it like to play harmonica?" one of the boys asked. "What's it like to be a star?"

Stone glanced up at the little ragamuffins in their tattered sheepskin tunics and their dirty faces. "Well," he said, "It's, it's..." Finding no words to express the joy, the disappointment, the pressures and the privileges of being a star, Stone placed his **G** harp to his puckered lips. "It's like this..." he said.

As the children looked on, Stone played the Basic Slant Up Riff, the easy run he had decided to use as the basis for the harp work on "Volcano Mouth."

Basic Slant Up Riff
④ ⑤ 6 ⑥

He started with the Note of Resolution, 4 draw, and slid the harp, without stopping his breath, to Wailing Note 5 draw. From here he played the 6 blow and wailed on the Wailing Note 6 draw.

"That sounds great!" the children cried. "Play some more!" To the sounds of clapping hands and shouts of "That's it, Stone, get down and boogie!" Stone played the Slant Down Riff.

Slant Down Riff
⑥ 6 ⑤④

"Yeah!" the kids shouted, "Get it on, Stone!" As Stone continued exploring the possibilities of Slant Harp, a little boy, no longer able to contain himself, started dancing. The other children formed a circle and clapped their hands.

Here are some of the Slant Harp Riffs Stone played. They are presented in diagrams so that, hopefully, you will play them, too.

To start out, Stone played the Ultra Slant Up and Down Riff. This run used the same idea as the Basic Slant, but enhanced the minor key sound even more.

Then Stone moved up an octave and played the Basic Slant Riff on holes 8, 9 and 10.

Now he switched to the Ultra Slant Up and Down Riff on holes 8, 9 and 10.

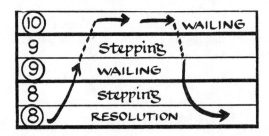

Amidst the handclapping, dancing and laughing, Stone decided to try an even more complex run. He would play a riff that went from Note of Resolution 4 draw up to Note of Resolution 8 draw.

"That's great!" the kids shouted. "Play some more." Stone looked at his watch. The show would be starting soon. He felt pretty confident that Slant Harp would do the trick on "Volcano Mouth," and he knew it was time to get inside the studio. But he couldn't tear himself away from the crowd of girls and boys who now were dancing with their hands in the air, their faces beaming.

"This is it," Stone thought. "This is why I wanted to be a good harmonica player. Not to become a star, not to become famous and make lots of money. No. I learned to play harp so I could bring joy and happiness into the world. So I could help people forget their problems. So I could make them feel good."

Inspired by this realization, Stone played the ultimate Slant Harp riff: the Slant Harp Scale.

Slant Harp Scale Up and Down
④⑤ 6 ⑥ 7 ⑧ 8 ⑨ 9 ⑩
⑩ 9 ⑨ 8 ⑧ 7 ⑥ 6 ⑤ ④

⑩	WAILING
9	Stepping
⑨	WAILING
8	Stepping
⑧	RESOLUTION
7	Stepping
⑦	Stepping
⑥	WAILING
6	Stepping
⑤	WAILING
5	Stepping
④	RESOLUTION

"Oh, wow!" the children shouted. "Wowwwwww!"

Now Stone wanted to really get down and play. Starting from the 4 draw, he played a long bending Note of Resolution, slipped to the 5 draw, the 6 blow, the 6 draw – wailing, warbling, tonguing, bending...

Then, the back door to the theatre suddenly opened, and the gruff face of the theatre manager appeared from the darkness. "Hey! You kids!" he shouted, "You get out of here or I'll call the police! You're making so much noise they can hear you inside." Then he spied Stone sitting beside the garbage cans. "And you, you old bum!" he spat at the greatest harp player who ever lived, "You get out of here, too. Shame on you for making these kids misbehave."

"But that's Stone!" a little girl shouted breathlessly. "That's the harp player for Umm and the Cave Boys."

The theatre manager moved closer. Catching a clearer glimpse of Stone's famous face, the theatre manager turned more colors than a smoggy sunset.

"Excuse me, Mr. Stone," he said, gruff voice now reduced to a whimpering falsetto. "I thought...I thought...oh well...you'd better come in right away. Everyone's looking for you. The show's about to start. Please, c'mon in. Please..."

Stone rose from his place behind the smelly cans. "And what about them?" he asked, pointing at the kids.

"What about them?" the manager asked.

"I want to play for them. I want to know I'm doing some good with all of this superstar hoopla."

"Well..." the theatre manager said. "I guess they can sit in the empty seats in the balcony."

"Whooppeeeee!" the children shouted.

The Show

The theatre's back stage was not as nice as the alley. The air was hot and stale, filled with the smells of sweat and makeup, B.O. and cologne.

"Right this way, Mr. Stone," said the theatre manager as he led the harp player past a line of scantily-dressed chorus girls. "Right this way."

Suddenly, Umm rushed up out of the darkness. "Stone!" she cried. She threw her arms around the harp man's neck. "Oh Stone, I was afraid you weren't going to show up. Listen, I don't care how your harp sounds. You're an important member of the Cave Boys. If you don't play, I don't sing."

Stone looked at her in surprise. "I thought nothing was more important to you than your career."

"You're just as important," Umm said. "And don't you forget it."

"You can say that again," added a familiar voice. It was Krok, holding his guitar. Behind him stood Gref and Smash.

"Hey," said Krok, "I'm sorry I got so uptight. This band wasn't any good 'til you joined it. You're playing harp with us – whether you want to or not."

"That's the way I feel too," said Gref.

"Me, too," added Smash.

"Okay," said the manager, "Enough of this emotion stuff. What's that have to do with rock and roll? You guys are ON!"

As the manager stepped to the side, the curtains rolled back and Stone suddenly realized that he was standing in front of 5,000 whistling, cheering people. As the cameras moved in, Dinah Sledge-hammer was saying, "And now, the group you've been waiting for, Umm and the Cave Boys."

Krok approached the microphone. "We wanna play a new song for you. This is 'Volcano Mouth'."

The Cave Boy guitarist rose his hand in a wide arc and brought it down on the **A** minor chord. The bass and drums kicked in. The rhythm had a jungle pulse, a primeval beat that made the bones shiver. Wearing a black and gold tiger fur mini dress, Umm danced across the stage. Hair swirling through the air, she grabbed the microphone and started to sing.

"Volcano mouth, volcano mouth
Your mouth is exploding!
                exploding!
                exploding!
Yeahhhhhhhhhhhhhhhhh!"

The people in the audience
looked at one another.
What was this music? What
did it mean? Some folks
stood up and waved their
arms. Others actually moved their hips, thighs, shoulders and hands to the infectious rhythm. Krok nodded at Stone and the harp man started to put what he had learned about Slant Harp into practice.

He wailed on 4 draw, slipped easily to 8 draw, back to 4 draw. He bent the 4 draw down, brought it back up, slid to 6 draw, blew on 7, sucked on 8, cascaded down to 4 draw in a minor key swirl of sound. His music was perfect for "Volcano Mouth."

Umm, Krok, Gref and Smash looked at Stone with relief and amazement. It was one thing to tell the Cave Boy harp player that he was more important to them than fame and success – quite another to believe it. But now they did believe it. Stone and his harmonica were incredible!

"Oh yeah!" the people in the audience shouted. This was the kind of music they'd always wanted to hear. Umm danced across the stage, whipping the mike cord behind her. Krok dipped to one knee and strummed his chords with robot-like precision. Gref and Smash grinned at one another and Stone wailed like a cave boy possessed.

What a show!

As the audience watched this spectacle of sound and movement, many found themselves thinking that Umm and the Cave Boys were like gods. Gods with the power to turn noise into music, silence into joy, boredom into excitement. And if not gods, then Umm and the Cave Boys were stars, stars as bright and beautiful as any in the heavens.

Few members of the audience realized they were watching the fruits of a long and often tedious labor, that Umm and the Cave Boys were like anyone else, that they fought and got angry with one another, that they were haunted by fears, frustrations, and deep, undefined yearnings for love and acceptance.

Fewer still realized that this vulnerability, this *humanity*, combined with a love for music, a capacity for joy and a need for self-expression, was the source of the magic that now filled the stage and seeped out into their lives. And almost no one was aware that the people themselves also were gods, goddesses, stars, heroes, heroines, what-have-you. No, the music was far too hot and the show too good for this kind of philosophizing.

Stone finished his solo to a standing ovation. Smash's drums rolled and thumped, stampeding the music into the second verse. The lyrics of the second verse were no more profound than those of the first. But who cared? All *anyone* heard was the pounding rhythm, the rich texture of Umm's voice, the razor-sharp slashes of Krok's guitar, the throbbing cry of Stone's harmonica.

Then, as quickly as the magic had begun, it stopped. The song was over. Band members hugged and shook hands. Applause washed over them like tumultuous waves of love.

"Umm and the Cave Boys!" Dinah Sledgehammer was shouting. "Umm and the Cave Boys!"

Krok grasped Stone's hand and looked him in the eye.

"Hey, man," he said, "that was the most incredible harp solo I ever heard you play."

The two musicians stood on the stage, the glow of their mutual success cutting through the rivalries, the arguments, the ego trips that had, for years, kept them from realizing how much they meant to each other.

"Tell me," Krok said. "How do you do it? How?"

"Talent," Stone said. "Sheer talent." Then the Cave Boy winked. "And a little help from my friends."

Notes

* SLANT HARP is a style of harmonica that sometimes sounds better than Cross Harp when accompanying songs in minor keys.

* The Slant Harp Formula is to count back two steps from the key the music is in. If the song is in the key of **B** minor COUNT BACK TWO STEPS (including the **B**) and play an **A** harp.

$$A \quad B \quad C \quad D \quad E \quad F \quad G$$
$$2 \quad 1$$

* When playing Slant Harp, the Notes of Resolution are 1 draw, 4 draw and 8 draw.

* Since Slant Harp is usually played on holes 4 draw and above, it works best on the lower-keyed harps such as **G** and **A**.

ELEVEN

Hubie's Blues or Everything I Almost Forgot to Put in the Book

So ends the saga of Stone, Umm, Krok, Gref and Smash. In Chapter XI, you and the author will meet an unforgettable character, learn some additional information on harp playing, and perhaps come to believe in a strange theory of musical reincarnation.

Hubie's Blues

Do you believe in reincarnation?

I didn't used to. Then I met Hubie. He was down at the bus station, sitting on his suitcase, softly playing the harmonica.

I couldn't hear him too well so I moved closer. He was playing a Cross Harp style. I recognized some of the riffs. The tone was familiar, too. Still, there was something special about this guy's playing. It had those extra touches of feeling and grace that distinguish a good harpist from a pro.

He looked at me through his dark glasses and said, "Hey! You're Gindick, aincha?"

"Sure am," I replied, flattered that a player this good would know who I am.

"Recognized you by your picture," he said. "Read your book, *The Natural Blues and Country Western Harmonica.*"

"What did you think?" I asked him.

"Good book for beginners. 'Course, no book is going to do it all. A guy or gal can know everything there is to know about the harp, and still not play it with any feeling."

"Unfortunately, you can't teach feeling," I said.

"Yeah, but you can encourage people to use feeling. Everybody's got it. It just comes out of some folks easier than others."

"Look," I said, "I'm writing a new book on harp playing. It's called *Rock n' Blues Harmonica.* I wonder if you'll take a look."

"Sure," he said.

"I got into my suitcase and pulled out the tattered manuscript I'd been working on for months. "This is it," I announced, and handed

188

it to him. I wondered if my new book had "feeling".

As he thumbed through the pages, I summarized the book for him. "It starts out telling people about the structure of music. Then it moves into the harmonica, explaining Straight Harp, Cross Harp and Slant Harp. Then it shows a bunch of riffs, how to play riffs in the I-IV-V progression, how to bend notes, how to use your hands..."

"Hmmmm," he said. "Looks pretty good, but I think you're leaving out some stuff people might want to know."

"Like what?" I asked, fighting the defensiveness that was creeping into my voice.

"Oh, stuff like using microphones and amps, the difference between using harp as a lead instrument and as a filler, playing harp and guitar at the same time, tongue blocking, good harp players to listen to."

"Guess I could add another chapter," I muttered.

"Yeah, write another chapter and name it after me. Name's Hubie." He held out his hand and we shook.

"I can see it now," he chuckled. "Everything I Forgot to Put in the Book or Hubie's Blues."

"Great title," I agreed.

"BUS 827 LEAVING IN 20 MINUTES FOR BAKERSFIELD," boomed a voice over the loud speaker.

Hubie looked at his watch. "Don't have much time," he said.

"Well, tell me what to write," I said, pulling out a pen and pad.

"Okay," Hubie said. "Let's start with microphones."

Sitting there on his suitcase, Hubie began explaining microphones to me. I wrote as fast as I could, and had some difficulty reading my writing later. Nonetheless, I think I got the gist of it.

Microphones and Amps

Although harp players are always looking for better ways to amplify their playing, it's pretty well established that the best way is to use a microphone. What mike you use and how you use it depends on the type of music you're playing and how you, the harp player, want to sound.

There are two basic approaches:

For rock and blues, you should cup your mike in your hands right along with your harmonica. When you can get the mike completely cupped, your tone will be especially rich and deep and will sound as much like a horn as like a harmonica.

For a country western style or for playing with an acoustic guitar, let the mike sit on a mike stand and play a few inches away. The harp sounds more like a harmonica when you do it this way. You also get better control over your volume because you can move closer or further away as you need to play louder or softer.

For the rock and blues style, you need a mike that fits easily in your hand and won't give feedback. Feedback is the high squeal you get when the sound coming through the amp is picked up by the mike. You can avoid feedback by not playing directly in front of your speaker, by setting the knobs on your amplifier or PA system to pick up the low tones (the bass) more than the treble, and by using an instrumental "flat" mike instead of a vocal mike.

When Hubie plays rock or blues he uses the Astatic, an old radio microphone that's hard to find in most music stores. He also uses The Green Bullet, a radio mike that's manufactured by the Shure Company. Other good harp mikes are Shure's PE 54D, PE 515, 56D and 588.

For the country western or accoustic style of amplification, Hubie uses a vocal microphone. This type of mike is "bright", designed to pick up the highs of a tone, as well as the lows. The vocal mike is more inclined to produce feedback, so it's important to make sure you're set up away from your speakers and don't have to play too loud.

190

When it comes to amplifiers, Hubie suggested an amp that has an active bass and treble control or graphic equalizer. These features let the harp player push or reduce the highs or lows of his harp's tone. This in turn lets the harpist adjust the tone to the sound he wants and cuts down on feedback.

He also recommends an amp with a gain control. The gain pushes the harp's tone into the amp. Playing with the gain up and the volume down produces a distorted, throaty tone often used by blues and rock players. Turning the volume up and the gain down results in a purer harmonica tone.

Another important feature in an amp is a "line out". This is a small jack in the back of the amplifier that allows the harp player to plug his amp directly into the public address system. It allows the harp player to play at high volume without having to worry about feedback or blowing up his amplifier.

When playing the country western style with the vocal mike, Hubie suggested plugging directly into the PA system the same way a vocalist would do.

"With this," he said, "You're not trying to change the tone of the harp. You simply want faithful reproduction."

Playing Guitar with Harp

Hubie looked at his watch. "Well, I got a few minutes left. Let me tell you about playing harp and guitar at the same time."

Scribbling furiously, I tried to get it all down.

Hubie said that harp playing often gets a person more interested and confident about music. This in turn leads to an interest in playing guitar.

A player should learn a few basic chords and chord progressions. Since the **C** harp is so popular, the beginning guitarist might want to learn some chords in the key of **G**. These would be **G, C** and **D**.

Of course, Hubie said, it's enough to know only **G** and **C**. If a person can get these two chords going on guitar, he can start playing two chord jams which is as good a way as any to begin.

Once there's some familiarity with a simple chord progression, all you have to do is put the right key harp in a harp rack (the best is made by the Elkin Company and is available in almost any music store) and start playing harp riffs to the chords. It takes time to learn to do two things at the same time, but it's not nearly as difficult as it seems.

Fills and Leads

"One thing you don't make very clear," Hubie said, "is the difference between fills and leads. And it's something *every* harp player should know."

Here's what Hubie had to say on the subject.

When playing with a guitarist and singer, the beginning harp player has a tendency to play constantly. Here's some guy or gal trying to keep a voice on key and the harp player is running up and down the scale playing licks.

When someone is singing, it's usually best to play riffs in between the singer's phrases. For instance, if the singer cries out, "My baby left me this morning. I've been crying all day long," the harp player should stick a short riff (or even a note) between the phrases instead of playing right through them. This keeps the voice and harp from constantly fighting with each other.

This is the way it would go:

Singer: "My baby left me this morning"
Harp: *"Wa wa wa."*
Singer: "I've been crying all day long"
Harp: *"Wa wa wa."*

On the other hand, when it's time for the harp player to take a lead, he should *take* it, stringing riffs together, building tension and momentum, playing with plenty of volume. Then, when the lead is over, the harp player should go back to playing fills that complement the singer's voice instead of compete with it.

When Not To Play Harp

"Some songs," said Hubie, "don't lend themselves to harp playing. The chord progression could be too complex. Or, it might be a song that features the guitar player.

"When the harp doesn't fit in, the harpist might do well to pick up a tambourine or other rhythm instrument."

"Then again, the harp player can find just one note, say 4 draw, or 3 blow – and play ONLY this note, finding a place where it adds support or interest and playing it there.

"If the harpist plays continuously, it can get boring. It's a lot better to leave people asking for more harmonica than to play it so much that they never want to hear harp again."

Tongue-Blocking

"You left out a pretty important harp playing technique," Hubie said.

"Oh yeah?" I asked. "What?"

"Tongue-blocking," he said. "The idea is that you make your mouth wide enough to play four holes, say 1,2,3 and 4 at the same time. Then you put the tip of your tongue on holes 2 and 3 and draw. The result is that you play holes 1 and 4. These are the same notes, only an octave apart."

Hubie pulled out his harp and showed me. The sound he played was like a chord, but also like a single note. I had heard this sound before but never incorporated it into my own playing.

"You can do this almost anywhere on your harp," Hubie said. "I like to do it on holes 1 and 4 because it represents the V chord of the

194

I-IV-V chord progression. It's a good technique for the semi-advanced harp player."

He played some blues licks, using that sweet tone that had first made me walk over to him in the bus station. I could hear his tongue-blocking technique and how it allowed him to play two holes at the same time. Hubie was right. I should have put it in the book. And now I would.

All Kinds of Chord Progressions

Hubie peered at me from behind his dark glasses. "I think you should mention that there are all kinds of chord progressions in today's rock and roll. The I-IV-V framework is just a jumping off spot for an infinite number of variations."

"Which ones do you think I should mention?" I asked.

Hubie then proceeded to list the wide variety of chord progressions. He said that the seventh chord is frequently used. He talked about relative minors. He said that the I chord could be an **A** minor and the next chord in the song would be a **B** minor. He went on and on.

"Of course, the specific chords of a song don't make that much difference to the harp player," he said. "The most important thing is that the song begins and ends on the I chord – that the music moves in a circle.

"Sometimes a song changes keys, so that the I chord becomes a **B** instead of an **A**, or a **C** instead of a **G**. When this happens, the harp player might need to pick up another key of harp – or just not play during that part of the song.

"For the most part, though, the harp player doesn't have to worry about what chords are played. Just play harp so it sounds good, and when it doesn't sound good, try to find out why."

Harp Players To Hear

"Look," Hubie said, "I realize that your book is more about what the guy or gal reading it can do with a harp than what other harp players have done.

"And I think that's a good idea. A harp player has to develop his own feeling, his own style, and learn to play harp from the ground floor up instead of hearing someone else and trying to imitate them. I recognize that that's the angle you're pushing in your book."

"Thanks," I said gratefully.

"Still," he said, "I think you should mention some of the hot harp players people can hear on records."

"Maybe you're right," I conceded.

"Tell people," said Hubie, "to listen to Paul Butterfield's early albums, to listen to John Mayall, to hear the stuff John Sebastion has done with the Lovin' Spoonful (especially "Night Owl Blues"). The *hard* blues players should hear Little Walter, Carey Bell, James Cotton, Walter Horton, Shakey Jake, Sonny Boy Williamson, Sonny Terry, Rod Piazza, Charlie Musselwhite, Magic Dick, Delbert McClinton, Corky Segal, Ken Shotmeyer to name must a few.

"Your country western fans should sit down with Charlie McCoy, and of course Willie Nelson's player, Mickey Raphael. If you got some guy out there who wants to hear how Cross Harp can be put together to play melodies, there's nobody better than these two.

"There are some rock bands who have guys who play harps as second instruments. Their playing may not be nothing fancy, but it's darn good. I'm thinking of the work Tom Johnston did when he was with Doobie Brothers. What's that song?"

"Long Train Running?" I asked.

"Yeah, that's it." Hubie said. "Another guy is Bruce Springsteen, and still another is Richard Davies who plays with SuperTramp. Pete Townsend does some interesting things, too.

196

"Rock's premier players are Norton Buffalo and Stevie Wonder. These guys play chromatic harps – much more complicated than the diatonic. Almost a different instrument. Does sound great though.

"Oh, yeah, Lee Oskar plays beautiful harmonica. Tell people to listen to his work with War, and also his solo albums...

"Who else...Bob Dylan, Donovan, Van Morrison, Toots Theilman, Larry Adler, Steve Forbert..."

"That's a pretty good list," I said. People were scurrying around the bus station, lugging suitcases, saying their goodbyes.

Hubie looked at his watch. "Well, I gotta go..."

"Play something first," I said. "Just a lick. I'd like to hear you once more."

Hubie looked at the entrance to the bus. He pulled out his harp and cupped it in his hands. *Waaaaaaa!* the harp moaned. *Waaaaaah Taa Waa Wa!*

Lord, it was sweet.

"And that," he said, "is Hubie's Blues."

He grabbed his suitcase and took a step toward the door. Then he stopped and shook my hand. He placed something hard and small in it. The next thing I knew he was out the door, climbing on the bus. The bus door closed and I watched him make his way down the crowded aisle and sit next to a fetching blonde who kissed him on the cheek. For a moment I wondered who she was. Exhaust shot from the rear of the bus and they were off.

Goodbye, Hubie, I said to myself. Thanks for your help.

I was walking, looking for the snack bar when I realized that my hand was clenched around something Hubie had given me. It was a small, strange harmonica. I'd never seen anything like it.

I played a 3 blow, a 4 draw, a 6 draw and a 9 blow. I played the Up and Down Blues Riff, I played the Six Blow Down. I played a Good

Morning Riff, I played the Good Morning Riff up to 3 draw, then 3 draw bent down. I couldn't stop playing!

The tone of this harmonica was incredible. It dripped like molasses, it soared like a rocket, it honked like a horn, it sang like a Streisand.

People were looking at me as my harp playing peaked on a bending 10 blow and tumbled through space, over the notes to the 2 draw. Some folks were smiling, tapping their feet. Others had disapproval on their faces.

Finally, I managed to wrestle the harmonica away from my lips. I looked at the harmonica more closely. Yes, this was it. This was the harmonica I'd been looking for all my life.

It was carefully carved from the tusk of a wild boar, and I felt sure that the reeds were from the hard bark of the boo boo tree.

Notes

* FEELING is more important to good music than technical skill, but technical skill never hurts.

* To play blues or rock harp, cup the microphone in your hands. For a more mellow, country-western sound, put the mike on a mike stand.

* When playing with other musicians, don't play constantly, but when it's your time to take the lead, GO FOR IT!

* Simple tonguing patterns on the SAME NOTE, say, 3 blow or 6 blow, usually sound better than complex riffs that go all over the scale.

* Rock music is usually MORE COMPLEX than the I-IV-V framework, but the same principles of harmonica accompaniment almost always apply.

* The more complex the music, the SIMPLER your harmonica playing should be.

Record Index

The following pages tell you what key of harmonica you need to jam with each song on over 75 popular records. The first key listed is for playing Straight Harp. The second key is for Cross Harp. Put a record on the turntable, find the right key of harp for the song you want to play, and begin molding harmonica sounds to the sounds of recorded music. Start with your Wailing Notes. Create tension until the music demands resolution. Resolve tension. Hey! You play pretty good!

Record Index

ALLMAN BROTHERS / EAT A PEACH

Ain't Wasting	B flat	E flat	Mountain Jam	E	A
Les Brers	A	D			
Melissa	E	A			
One Way Out	A	D	Mountain Jam	E	A
Trouble	A	D			
Standback	E	A			
Blue Sky	E	A			
Little Martha	E	A			

JOAN ARMATRADING / TO THE LIMIT

Barefoot	E	A	Bottom	B flat	E flat
Letter	C	F	Up Town	C	F
Am I Blue	D	G	Do You	E	A
You Rope	B flat	E flat	Wishing	D	G
Baby I	G	C	Let It	E	A

JOAN ARMATRADING / ME, MYSELF, I

Me	E	A	Kisses	E	A
Ma Me	E	A	America	E	A
Friends	E flat	A flat	Heart	A	D
Tomorrow	G	C	Simon	B	E
Light	G	C	Need	C	F

---

* When the Straight Harp key doesn't work, it may be because the song is in a minor key. To find out what the relative major is, count up 3 from the Straight Harp listing, and play Straight Harp in a harmonica of that key.

A	B	C
1	2	3

Or

B	C	D
1	2	3

202

ATLANTIC RHYTHM SECTION / UNDERDOG

Do It Or Die	D	G	Time Left	D	G
Born Ready	A	D	Only Music	E	A
Hate the Blues	G	C	Spooky	E	A
Get Stoned	G	C	My Song	E	A
Indigo Passion	G	C			

PAT BENATAR / IN THE HEAT OF THE NIGHT

Heartbreaker	F	B flat	Live For Love	D flat	F sharp
Need A Lover	F	B flat	Rated X	E	A
If You Think	G	C	Don't Let	A	D
In the Heat	D flat	F sharp	No You Don't	B	E
My Clone	F	B flat	So Sincere	F	B flat

ELVIN BISHOP / STRUTTING MY STUFF

Strutting	D	G	Holler	B	E
Hey, Hey	D	G	Slick Titty	D	G
My Girl	E	A	Grab Love	A	D
Love	G	C	Good Time	C	F
Fooled Around	F	G flat	Joy	C	F

BLONDIE / PARALLEL LINES

Telephone	B	E	11:59	G	C
One Way	E flat	A flat	Anything	B flat	E flat
Picture	A flat	D flat	Sunday	E flat	A flat
Fadaway	B flat	E flat	Heart	F	B flat
Pretty Baby	A flat	D flat	Gonna Love	B flat	A flat
I Know	B flat	A flat	Go Away	C	F

BLUES BROTHERS / MADE IN AMERICA

Soulfinger	B	E	Green Onions	F	B flat
Who's Making	F	B flat	Ain't Got You	E	A
Do You Love	D	G	Bottom	A	D
Guilty	A	D	Miami	G	C
Perry Mason	C	F			
Cell Block	C	F			

BLUES BROTHERS / BRIEFCASE FULL OF BLUES

Can't Turn	C	F	Groove Me	A	D
Bartender	C	F	Don't Know	G	C
Messin'	B	E	Soul Man	F	B flat
Almost	E	A	B Movie	E	A
Biscuit	F	B flat	Flip Flop	B flat	E flat
Shot Gun	B flat	E flat	Turn You	C	F

KARLA BONOFF

Trouble	A	D	Baby Don't Go	C	F
Restless	A	D	Never Stop	D	G
The Letter	G	C	Loving You	E	A
You Walk	D	G	Water Wide	D	G
A Fool	A	D			

JACKSON BROWNE / HOLD OUT

Disco	C	F	Missing Persons	C	F
Hold Out	C	F	A Loan	F sharp	B flat
That Girl	D	G	Hold On	A	D
Boulevard	A	D			

JACKSON BROWNE / THE PRETENDER

The Fuse	G	C	Only Child	F	B flat
Bright Baby	F sharp	B	Daddy's Tune	C	F
Linda	B	E	Sleep's Gate	A	D
Here Come	B flat	E flat	The Pretender	G	C

JIMMY BUFFETT / CHANGES IN LATTITUDES

Changes	D	G	Margaritaville	D	G
Wonder	G	C	Shelter	E	A
Bananna	G	C	Miss You	C	F
Tampico	A	D	Biloxi	A	D
Lovely	C	F	Landfall	G	C

NORTON BUFFALO / LOVIN' IN THE VALLEY OF THE MOON

Lovin	G	C	Hangin'	D	G
One Kiss	G	C	Another	F	B flat
Ghetto	A flat	D flat	Rosalie	F	B flat
Nobody	E	A	Jig's Up	A	D
Puerto	E	A	Eighteen	E	A
			Sea	C	F

PAUL BUTTERFIELD / BETTER DAYS

New Blues	G	C	Baby	E	A
Send Me	A flat	D flat	Buried	A	D
Baby's Heart	F	B flat	Rule	E	A
Wrong	F	B flat	Nobody	C	F

B 52's

Planet Claire	E	A	Lava	E	A
52 Girls	A	D	Hero	A	D
Dance	B flat	E flat	6062	B	E
Rock Lobster	C	F			

J.J. CALE

Lies	C	F	Ridin'	F	B flat
Everything	F	B flat	Going Down	A	D
Kiss Wind	B	E	Soulin'	E	A
Changes	D	G	Playing	G	C
Right	B	E	Mojo	E	A
Oklahoma	A	D	Louisianna	A	D

KIM CARNES / MISTAKEN IDENTITY

Bette Davis	F	B flat	Rules	G	C
Hit and Run	B	E	Hold On	D flat	F sharp
Identity	F	B flat	Call It	F	B flat
Away	E	A	Pals	C	F
Cards	D	G			

THE CARS / THE CARS

Good Times	B	E	All	B	E
Best Friend	F	B flat	Bye Bye	E	A
What I Needed	E	A	Movin'	E	A
In Touch	D flat	F sharp	Mixed Up	A	D
Don't Stop	A	D			

RY COODER / PARADISE AND LUNCH

Tamp em'	D	G	Cigarette	E flat	A flat
Tattler	F	B flat	Feelin'	E flat	A flat
Married	E	A	Walls	C	F
Jesus	C	F	Mexican	E flat	A flat
All Over	C	F	Ditty	C	F

RY COODER

Bourgeois	G	C	Smack Dab	F	B flat
Got Mine	E	A	Stand	G	C
Lift Up	D	G	Roses	B	E
He'll Go	F	B flat	Chloe	B	E
			Irene	E	A

RY COODER / JAZZ

Bad Bill	E	A	Mist	D	G
Face To Face	D flat	F sharp	Flashes	E flat	A flat
Pearls	F sharp	B	Davenport	G	C
The Dream	F	B flat	Shine	G	C
Meeting	D flat	F sharp	Nobody	G	C
			Happy	F	B flat

RY COODER / BOP TIL YOU DROP

Sister	B flat	E flat	Hollywood	C	F
Go Home	E flat	A flat	Granny	A flat	D flat
Makes You Rich	D flat	F sharp	Trouble	F	B flat
Work Out	E	A	Mess Up	D	G
			Win	F sharp	B

ELVIS COSTELLO / THIS YEAR'S MODEL

No Action	E	A	Hand	A	D
This Year's	D	G		D	G
The Beat	B	E	Lip	E	A
Pump It	B	E	Paradise	D	G
Triggers	F	B flat	Lipstick	B	E
Belong	D	G	Radio	E	A

ELVIS COSTELLO

Working	E	A	Red Shoes	E	A
Miracle	E	A	Zero	F	B flat
Dancing	D	G	Mystery	G	C
Cain	G	C	Pay Back	G	C
Alison	E	A	Not Angry	E	A
Sneaky	G	C	World	G	C
Detectives	C	F			

RODNEY CROWELL / BUT WHAT WILL NEIGHBORS THINK

80's	D	G	Ashes	G	C
Money	F sharp	B	Heartbroke	D	G
Feeling	C	F	Queen	A	D
Rock	A	D	Blues	G	C
Good Night	G	C	England	E flat	A flat

DIRE STRAITS / MAKING MOVIES

Tunnel	D	G	Espresso	G	?
Romeo	F	B flat	Hand	C	F
Skateaway	G	C	Solid Rock	A	D
			Les Boys	D	G

BOB DYLAN / HIGHWAY 61 REVISITED

Rolling Stone	C	F	Queen Jane	C	F
Tombstone	C	F	Highway 61	B flat	E flat
Train	A flat	D flat	Tom Thumb	G	C
Buick 6	C	F	Desolation Row	E	A
Thin Man	D	G			

BOB DYLAN / BLOND ON BLOND

Rainy Day	E	A	I Want You	F	B flat
Pledging	A	D	Memphis Blues	E	A
Visions	A	D	Pillbox Hat	A	D
Sooner or Later	F	B flat	Like A Woman	E	A
Your Way	G	C	Sad Eyed	D	G
Achilles	G	C			
Sweet Marie	D	G			
Fourth Time	E	A			
5 Believers	A	D			

DOOBIE BROTHERS / GREATEST HITS

China Grove	E	A	Jesus	A	D
Long Train	G	C	Runnin'	E	A
Streets	C	F	Midnight	G	C
Listen Music	E	A	Take Me	A	D
Back Water	D	G	Without	E	A
Highway	A	D			

DOOBIE BROTHERS / MINUTE BY MINUTE

Song			Song		
Fool Believes	D flat	F sharp	Sweet Feelin'	A	D
Minute By	G	C	Steamer	G	C
Depending	A	D	Never Change	C	F
			Fool Survives	F	B flat

JOE ELY / MUSTA NOTTA GOTTA LOTTA

Song			Song		
Musta	E	A	Paid	E	A
Dallas	E	A	Rockin'	D	G
Wishing	G	C	Livin	E	A
Hold On	A	D	Road	E	A
Rock Me	E	A	Heart	C	F
			Bet Me	E	A

STEVE FORBERT / ALIVE ON ARRIVAL

Song			Song		
Laurel	D	G	Big City	F	B flat
Toast	D	G	Grand Central	D	G
Thinkin	E	A	Tonight	C	F
What Guy	E	A	Settle Down	B flat	E flat
Gonna Be	D	G	Cannot Win	B	E

STEVE FORBERT / JACKRABBIT SLIM

Song			Song		
Romeo	A	D	So Real	D	G
Sweet	D flat	F sharp	Baby	F	B flat
Love	B	E	Complicate	A	D
Little Jo	A	D	Soap	A	D
Wait	D	G	January	B flat	E flat

THE J. GEILS BAND / FREEZE FRAME

Song			Song		
Freeze	C	F	Flame	C	F
Rage	G	C	River	G	C
Centerfold	G	C	Angel	E	A
Remember	A flat	D flat	Wall	A	D
Insane	C	F			

J. GEILS / LADIES INVITED

No Wrong	A	D	The Lady	C	F
Can't Go	C	F	Baby	G	C
Lay Down	C	F	Diddy Bop	G	C
Thinking	A	D	Romance	C	F
No Doubt	E	A	Chimes	C	F

J. GEILS / "LIVE" FULL HOUSE

Purse	C	F	Serves You	E	A
Homework	D	G	Cruising	A	D
Pack Fair	C	F	Looking	C	F
Whammer Jam	E	A			
Hard Driven	D	G			

BEST OF THE J. GEILS BAND

Southside	G	C	Detroit	C	F
Give It	G	C	Whammer	E	A
Where Did	A	D	I Do	G	C
House Party	E	A	Musta Got	C	F
			Looking	C	F

EMMY LOU HARRIS / BLUE KENTUCKY GIRL

Sisters Coming	D	G	Sorrow	B	E
Waters	D	G	Love Me	D	G
Rough A ?	D	G	You Leave	B flat	E flat
Hickory Wind	F	B flat	Kentucky	F	B flat
Last Dance	B flat	E flat	Cowgirls	E flat	A flat

BIG WALTER HORTON

Good Time	G	C	Tell Me	E	A
Christine	G	C	Mercy	D	G
Lovin'	E	A	That Ain't	E	A
Boy Blue	F	B flat	Temptation	E	A
Can't Hold	E	A	Trouble	A	D
Sun	G	C			

IRON CITY ROCKERS / HAVE A GOOD TIME

Song			Song		
Good Time	A	D	Not Dead	A	D
Push	G	C	Blondie	A	D
Pumping	G	C	Old Man	A	D
Hypnotized	A	D	Junior	E	A
Love	C	F	Runnin'	G	C
Angela	A	D	Rick	G	C

JOE JACKSON / LOOK SHARP

Song			Song		
One More Time	E flat	A flat	Baby	G	C
Sunday Papers	E	A	Look Sharp	C	F
Is She?	B flat	E flat	Fools In Love	E	A
Happy Love	G	C	Instant Mash	G	C
Throw It Away	A	D	Pretty Girls	A	D

JOE JACKSON / JUMPIN' JIVE

Song			Song		
Jumpin'	A flat	D flat	Jive	F	B flat
Dead	B flat	E flat	Mouth	B flat	E flat
Is You	A	D	Sober	E flat	A flat
The Cats	B flat	E flat	Meat	E flat	A flat
San Fran	F	B flat	Tuxedo	E flat	A flat
Mop	B flat	E flat	Must I?	B flat	E flat

BILLY JOEL / 52nd STREET

Song			Song		
Big Shout	G	C	Stiletto	F	B flat
Honesty	B flat	E flat	Rosalinda	G	C
My Life	D	G	Mile	B flat	
Zanzibar	C	F	The Night	C	F
			52nd Street	G	C

BILLY JOEL / THE STRANGER

Song			Song		
Movin	F sharp	B	Vienna	B flat	E flat
Stranger	E	A	The Good	C	F
The Way	D	G	She's Always	E flat	A flat
Italian	G	C	Get It	F	B flat
			Everybody	D	G

RICKI LEE JONES

Chuck E.	A	D	All Star Joint	E	A
Saturday	A	D	Coolsville	B	E
Night Train	E	A	Weasle	A	D
Young Blood	F	B flat	Company	C	F
Easy Money	D	G	Hours	C	F
Texaco	F sharp	B			
	G	C			

ALBERT KING / I'LL PLAY THE BLUES FOR YOU

Blues	G	C	Doggone	G	C
Brother	B flat	E flat	Laundromat	A	D
Somebody	D	G	Burn Down	A flat	D flat
Loving	G	C	Angel	A flat	D flat

KINGFISH

Lightnin'					
Supplication	D	G	Honor	E	A
Northland	E	A	Iron	F	B flat
Asia	E	A	Time	E	A
Home	A	D	Hypno	E	A
Joy	E	A	Bye	A	D

LED ZEPPELIN II

Whole Lotta	E	A	Heartbreaker	A	D
What Is	E	A	Loving	A	D
Lemon Song	E	A	Ramble On	E	A
Thanks	D	G	Moby	D	G
			Bring It	E	A

GORDON LIGHTFOOT / COLD ON THE SHOULDER

Water	F sharp	B	Weak	F	B flat
Rainy	B	E			
Shoulder	G	C	Fine	E flat	A flat
Rock	B	E	Cherokee	F sharp	B
Bells	F	B flat	Now	D	G
Trout	E	A	Slide	B	E

DAVID LINDLEY / EL RAYO X

Romeos	B flat	E flat	El Rayo	A flat	D flat
Bye Bye	C	F	Ol' Lady	A flat	D flat
Mercury	F	B flat	Look	D flat	F sharp
Quarter	A	D	Petit	A	D
Ain't Way	C	F	Sinus	D flat	F sharp
Twist	D flat	F sharp	Pay	E flat	A flat

LITTLE FEAT / THE LAST RECORD ALBUM

Romance	D	G	One Love	E	A
Dream	E	A	Borderline	D	G
Distance	G	C	Somebody	E flat	A flat
Day	E	A			

KENNY LOGGINS / CELEBRATE ME HOME

Lady	F	B flat	Dreams	E	A
Be Wise	D	G	Melody	E	A
Believe	D	G	Celebrate	F	B flat
Set Free	A	D	Daddy	G	C
Lie	B flat	E flat	Know Me	G	C

DELBERT McCLINTON / SECOND WIND

B Movie	E	A	Watcha	E	A
Isn't So	B flat	E flat	Sick	G	C
Corina	B flat	E flat	Someday	C	F
Easy	B flat	F flat	River	G	C
Spoonful	E	A	Lovinest	E	A

CHARLIE McCOY / GOOD TIME CHARLIE – FASTEST HARP

Good Time	G	C	Henry	A	D
San Antone	A	D	Get It Right	A flat	D flat
Soul Song	G	C	Louisianna	A	D
Something	A	D	Shenandoah	D flat	F sharp
Minor	A	D	Orange Blossom	C	F
Touch	D	G			

Silver	E	A	Release Me	D	G
Why Me	A	D	Rollin'	B	E
Paper Roses	A flat	D flat	Closed Doors	E flat	A flat
Sunshine	B	E	Tribute	D	G
Persuaded	G	C	Ruby	G	C
Fastest Harp	B	E			

CHARLIE McCOY / THE REAL McCOY

Today I Started	F sharp	B	Lovin Her	A	D
Orange Blossom	C	F	Easy Lovin'	B flat	E flat
Only Daddy	E	A	How Can I	C	F
Jackson	C	F	Help Me	E	A
Hangin' On	E	A	Country Road	C	F
Real McCoy	B	E			

MARK-ALMOND / TO THE HEART

State of Mind	E flat	A flat	One More	C	F
Return	E flat	A flat	Busy	A	D
Here Comes	A	D	Everybody	E flat	A flat
Trade Wind	G	C			

MARK-ALMOND / OTHER PEOPLES' ROOMS

The City	D	G	Lonely People	A	D
Girl	A	D	Just A Friend	D	G
Look Like	E flat	A flat	Then I Have	B flat	E flat
Other Rooms	C	F	Vivaldi	F	B flat

TAJ MAHAL / GIANT STEP

Giant Step	D	G	Six Days	C	F
Woman	G	C	Farther	A	D
School Girl	D	G	Hands Off	D	G
Somebody	G	C	Bacon Fat	C	F

TAJ MAHAL / DE OL' FOLKS AT HOME

Linin'Track	D	G	Aristocracy	C	F
Country Blues	D flat	F sharp	Blind Boy	B	E
Ox Moan	D flat	F sharp	Stagger Lee	D flat	F sharp
Rain Blues	C	F	Cajun Tune	B flat	E flat
Soulful Tune	C	F	Fishin'	D	G
Candy Man	C	F	Annie's Lover	B	E
Cluck	C	F			

BOB MARLEY AND THE WAILERS / CATCH A FIRE

Concrete Jungle	E	A	Stir It Up	A	D
Slave Driver	D	G	Kinky Reggae	A	D
400 Years	B flat	E flat	No More	A	D
Stop That Train	G	C	Midnight	A	D
Baby, Date	A	D			

BOB MARLEY AND THE WAILERS / RASTAMAN VIBRATIONS

Positive	A	D	Crazy Baldhead	A	D
Roots, Rock	B	E	Cap Fit	B flat	E flat
Johnny Was	A	D	Night Shift	D	G
Cry To Me	C	F	War	B flat	E flat
Want More	D	G	Rat Race	B flat	E flat

BOB MARLEY / NATTY DREAD

Lively Up	D	G	So Jah	D	G
No Woman	C	F	Natty	A	D
Belly Full	C	F	Bend Down	C	F
Rebel	A	D	Talkin'	A	D
			Revolution	C	F

JOHN MAYALL / USA UNION

Nature	B	E	Legs	G	C
Crazy	C	F	Car	E flat	A flat
Night	F	B flat	Crying	E	A
Road	F sharp	B	Pretty	A flat	D flat
Possessive	A	D	Deep Sea	DaG	

JOHN MAYALL / TURNING POINT

Laws Change	C	F	California	D	G
Saw Mill	E	A	Roxanne	C	F
Gonna Fight	B	E	Room To Move	D flat	F sharp
Hard Share	G	C			

STEVE MILLER / NUMBER 5

Good Morning	A	D	Mexico	G	C
I Love You	D	G	Midnight	C	F
Country	D	G	Complex	D	G
Chili	C	F	Jackson	D	G
Tokens			Never Kill	D	G

STEVE MILLER / FLY LIKE AN EAGLE

Fly	A	D	Take Money	G	C
Honey	B	E	Rock Me	B	E
Serenade	C	F	Send Me	G	C
Dane	G	C	Odyssey	G	C
Mercury	F sharp	B	Marie	D	G
			Window	G	C

VAN MORRISON / WAVELENGTH

Kingdom Hall	A	D	Wavelength	C	F
Check It	G	C	Santa Fe	A	D
Natalie	D	G	Hungry	A flat	D flat
Venice	G	C	Take It	A	D
Lifetimes	A flat	D flat			

VAN MORRISON / ASTRAL WEEKS

Astral Weeks	A	D	Young Lovers	A	D
Beside You	G	C	Madam George	G	C
Sweet Thing	E	A	Ballerina	G	C
Cyprus Ave.	B flat	E flat	Slim Slow	G	C

VAN MORRISON BAND AND STREET CHOIR

Domino	A	A	Blue Money	A	D
Crazy	C	F	Virgo	E	A
Kiss	A	D	Gypsy	C	F
Working	G	C	Janine	E	A
Dreamland	A	D	Need Some	G	C
Lover	G	C	Street	E	A

MOTELS

Anticipating	A	D	Atomic	B	E
Kix	B	E	Celia	A	D
Total Control	D	G	Porn	E	A
Love Help	C	F	Dressing	E	A
Bullets	D	G	Counting	C	F

WILLIE NELSON / WILLIE NELSON SINGS KRISTOFFERSON

Bobbie McGee	A	D	Show Me	E	A
Help Me	D	G	Lovin Her	E	A
Pilgrim			Sunday	C	F
Why Me	A	D	Story Ends	A	D
Good Times	A	D			

WILLIE NELSON / STARDUST

Stardust	G	C	Sept. Song	A flat	D flat
Georgia	D flat	F sharp	Sunny Side	G	C
Blue Skies	C	F	Moonlight		
All of Me	G	C	Get Around	A	D
Unchained	G	C	Someone	A	D

WILLIE NELSON & LEON RUSSELL / ONE FOR THE ROAD

Detour	D	G	Don't Fence	D	G
Saw The Light	G	C	Wild Side	E	A
Heartbreak	D	G	Canyon	A	D
World Go By	E	A	Sioux	G	C
Trouble	A	D	Sunshine	F	B flat

QUARTERFLASH

Harden	D	E	Right Love	D	E
Fool	D	E	Deuce	G	C
Critical	A	D	Kind	B flat	E flat
Valerie	C	F	Avenue	G	C
True	D	G		B flat	E flat

LEE OSKAR / BEFORE THE RAIN

Before Rain	D flat	F sharp	Feeling	E	A
Steppin'	B flat	E flat	Words	C	F
SF Bay	D flat	F sharp	Sing Song	D flat	F sharp
			Haunted	C	F

ROBERT PALMER / PRESSURE DROP

Give an Inch	B flat	E flat	Here With You	A	D
Work	E	A	Trouble	D	G
Arms	D	G	Fine Time	A	D
Riverboat	B flat	E flat	Which	A	D
Pressure Drop	G	C			

BONNIE RAITT / SWEET FORGIVENESS

Leave Home	D	G	Forgive	B flat	E flat
Runaway	C	F	Farewell	B flat	E flat
Two Lives	F	B flat	Three	B	E
Louise	A	D	Time	B	E
Gamblin'	D	G	Home	E	A

ROCKPILE / SECONDS OF PLEASURE

Teacher	C	F	Wrong Again	D	G
Sugar	E	A	Pet You	D	G
Heart	A	D			
	B flat	E flat	Thrill	A	D
Now	A	D	Book	A	D
Knife	E	A	Fool	C	F
Fast Thing	C	F	Nothin'	A	D

ROLLING STONES / SOME GIRLS

Miss You	A	D	Faraway Eyes	F	B flat
Whip	A	D	Respectable	A	D
Imagination	A	D	Run	G	C
Girls	A	D	Beast	E	A
Lies	A	D	Shattered	A	D

ROLLING STONES / TATTOO YOU

Start Me Up	A	B flat	Worried	C	F
Hang Fire	A	D	Top	B flat	E flat
Slave	B	E	Heaven	D flat	F sharp
Little	F	B flat	No Use	E	A
Limo	G	C	Waiting	C	F
Neighbors	E	A			

THE SIEGEL SCHWALL BAND / 953 WEST

Spend Time	E	A	Time	G	C
Traitor	E	A	Denver		
Good Woman	G	C	Wine	E	A
Country	G	C	Reed	G	C
Drinking	E	A	Blowout	C	F

PAUL SIMON / ONE TRICK PONY

Late	F	B flat			
God Movies	E	A	Ace in the Hole	A	D
One Trick	A	D	Nobody	E flat	A flat
Heart			God Bless	F	B flat
Marion	B	E	Long, Long	F sharp	B

BRUCE SPRINGSTEEN / GREETINGS FROM ASBURY PARK

BLinded	E	A	Angel	G	C
Growing Up	C	F	For You	F	B flat
Arkansas	D	G	Spirit	E	A
Bus Stop	G	C	Saint	A	D
Flood	G	C			

BRUCE SPRINGSTEEN / DARKNESS ON EDGE OF TOWN

Badlands	E	A	Promised Land	G	C
Adam	E	A	Factory	C	F
Something	G	C	Streets	A	D
Candy	C	F	Prove It	A	D
Racing	F	B flat	Darkness	G	C

SOUTHSIDE JOHNNY & THE ASBURY JUKES / THIS TIME ITS FOR REAL

This Time	G	C	Some Things	E	A
Without Love	F	B flat	Little Girl	E	A
Popeye	C	F	Fever	A	D
First Night	C	F	Love	G	C
	D flat	F sharp	Dance	G	C
She's Got	A	D			

SUPERTRAMP / CRIME OF THE CENTURY

School	A	D	Dreamer	G	C
Bloody Well	B flat	E flat	Rudy	B flat	E flat
Hide	F	B flat	Everyone	B flat	E flat
Asylum	B flat	E flat	Crime	C	F

GEORGE THOROGOOD / MORE GEORGE THOROGOOD

I'm Wanted	C	F	Tip On	E	A
Philly	E	A	Goodbye	D	G
Ticket	E	A	Blue	C	F
Bottom	A	D	Make It	B	E
Night Time	A	D	Restless	E	A

UMM AND THE CAVE BOYS / FUNKY FOSSILS

Tango Tarpits	G	C	Volcano Mouth	A	D
12 Bars	E	A	Funky Dinosaur	B	E
Eat It	C	F	Cave Angel	C	F

WET WILLIE / DRIPPIN' WET

All Right	C	F	Airport	C	F
Katy	A	D	Blind	G	C
Woman	A	D	Blues	C	F
Hot Chick	E	A	Bamalama	F	B flat

STEVIE WONDER / HOTTER THAN JULY

Hear	E	A	Blaster	C	F
All I Do	B	E	Like You	A flat	D flat
Rocket	B	E	Cash	D	G
Stand	A	D	Lately	F sharp	B
You Could	A	D	Happy	C	F

NEIL YOUNG / HAWKS AND DOVES

Little Wing	B flat	E flat	Staying	G	C
Homestead	D	G	Coastline	C	F
In Space	C	F	Man	G	C
Kennedy	F	B flat	Coming	G	C
			Jawks	G	C

WARREN ZEVON / EXCITABLE BOY

Johnny's Band	A	D	Night	B flat	E flat
Excitable	E	A	Vera	C	F
Roland	B	E	Tenderness	E	A
Werewolves	G	C	Lawyers	A	D
Martyr	F	B flat			

Krok's Favorite Guitar Chords

"What about me?" asked Krok. "Don't I get in this book of yours?"
O.K. Krok. Simmer down.

Here are some of Krok's favorite chord progressions. They are the
easiest chords known to music. Simply push down the strings as
indicated by the dots, and strum with your fingers or flatpick in your
other hand. The X means *don't* strum this string. The O means *do*
strum this string even though you aren't pressing it down. If your
fingers hurt, apply a liquid bandage (also known as "Clear Skin") to
your fingertips. This will deaden the feeling.

The first progression is Krok's "Old 50's Ballad Music." It's in the key
of **G.** Moving smoothly from one to the next, give each chord 2 or 4
strums. When you get to the **D** chord, return to the **G** and start the
progression again.

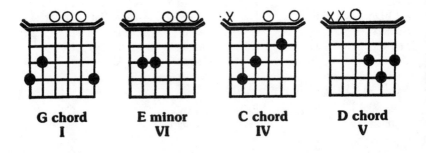

| G chord | E minor | C chord | D chord |
| I | VI | IV | V |

To accompany this progression with harmonica, play Straight Harp
with a **G** harmonica, Cross Harp with a **C** harmonica, and Slant
Harp with a harp in the key of **F.**

Here's the same progression in the key of **C.** Play Straight Harp with
a **C** harmonica, Cross Harp with an **F** harp, and Slant Harp on your
B flat harmonica.

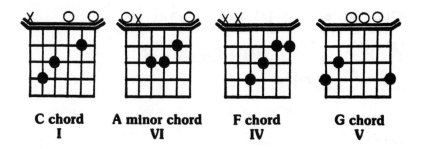

C chord	A minor chord	F chord	G chord
I	VI	IV	V

Here's one of the easiest jams ever. It's in the key of **E minor**. Simply go back and forth between your **E minor** chord and your **A** chord. Give each chord either 2 or 4 beats.

E minor chord	A chord
I	IV

Play Cross Harp to this progression with an **A** harp, Slant Harp with a **D** harp. To play Straight Harp, count up 3 steps from the **E minor** to the **G**, and play a **G** harp.

The last of Krok's favorite progressions is in **A minor.** Play the **A minor** for 4 strums, **F** for 4 strums, and **G** for 4 strums. Return to the **A minor** and play the cycle again, and again.

A minor chord	F chord	G chord

Play Cross Harp with a **D** harmonica, Slant Harp with a **G** harmonica. To play Straight Harp, count up 3 steps from the **A minor**, and play a **C** harp.

The Natural Blues & Country Western Harmonica Book and Cassette

Got an urge to play the blues?

The Natural Blues and Country Western Harmonica is a 130 page book and 66 minute cassette that will get you wailing and warbling – even if you know nothing about music.

The book starts with a step-by-step guide to buying your harmonica, holding it, putting it in your mouth. Then it introduces you to the most easily understood method of playing blues harp ever devised.

Included are:
- Simple diagrams of the basic riffs of blues harmonica.
- Illustrations showing which notes on your harmonica always harmonize with each other and with guitar music, and which ones don't.
- A glossary explaining every musical term used in the book.
- A record index telling what key of harmonica you need to accompany each song on 100 widely owned record albums.
- A collection of 25 melodies – the kind you might play around a campfire.

And that's only the book!

The 66 minute cassette lesson gives you slow-motion, play-along examples of every riff and technique described in the book. Also important – there's lots of easy guitar music for you to accompany with your C harp.

Together, this book and cassette provide the information you need to start playing your harp AND the opportunity for actual playing experience. If you've got an urge to play the blues, send for The Natural Blues & Country Western Harmonica book and cassette today. **Only $11.95.**